20/20 VISION

A Focus on the Future of the Real Estate Industry

Charles M. Dahlheimer

co-author of
Real Estate in the '90s:
A Whole New World Ahead

A road map routing
the serious-minded real estate professional
through challenging and
potentially profitable times
in the Whole New World of
Real Estate in the Twenty-First Century

Courtesy of the

MICHIGAN
Association of **REALTORS®**

Printed in the United States of America

Cover Design: Gail M. Wright

ISBN 0-9623018-3-3

Single copy price: $24.95 US; $37.50 Canadian

North American Consulting Group publications are available at special quantity discounts for use in educational programs or in corporate promotions. Please contact the publisher for additional information.

Published by
North American Consulting Group, Inc.
P.O. Box 2096, St. Louis, MO 63158
314-664-8552 Fax: 314-664-6310
e-mail: info@nacgonline.com

visit our Web site at: www.nacgonline.com

Dedicated to
My Wife, Linda,
Our Son, Michael,
and our special friends
Ursa, Sophie and Phoebe

Acknowledgements

Over the years, the participants in our Great Idea Conferences have provided unique and valuable insights into the developing trends in the residential real estate arena. We wish to express our sincere appreciation especially to the following broker-owners and executives who participated in our 1998-99 focus on "The Real Estate Company of the Future."

Brian and Joan Allen, Windermere Cronin & Caplan, Portland, OR; Angela Anderson, Daniel Gale Real Estate, Long Island, NY; Mo Anderson, Keller Williams Realty, Austin, TX; Leslie Appleton-Young, California Assn. of Realtors, Los Angeles, CA; Richard Baker, Jr., The Danberry Company, Toledo, OH; Lynn Beckenhauer, Dilbeck Realtors BH&G, LaCanada, CA; Greg Benner, Tomlinson Black South, Inc., Spokane, WA; Mike Borschuk, Century 21 Market Place, Sioux City, IA; Daniel Bourgoin, Microsoft HomeAdvisor, Redmond, WA; Gilbert P. Bricault, J. W. Riker, Warwick, RI; Peter Burgdorff, ERA Franchise Systems, Inc., Parsippany, NJ; Laura Buser, Prudential Real Estate Affiliates, Irvine, CA; Tim Corliss, Senior Advantage Real Estate Council, Murphys, CA; Richard D. Cosner, The Prudential California Realty, Riverside, CA; Nina Cottrell, Council of Residential Specialists, Chicago, IL; Gary Daniels, Harmon Publishing, Dallas, TX; Ed DesRoches, Wellesley Publications, Needham, MA; Gregory P. Donovan, Cendant Corporation, Parsippany, NJ; Thomas W. Dooley, TWD & Associates, Arlington Heights, IL; Shannon Elam, Pen West Assn. of Realtors, Los Altos, CA; Chris Elliott, Image Maker Systems, Cayucos, CA; Mark Everett, HMS Southwest, Scottsdale, AZ; Roy Fair, Realty Executives of Illinois, Aurora, IL; Bridget Gardner, The Prudential Real Estate Affiliates, Irvine, CA; John Geha, Growth Management Systems, Inc., Toledo, OH; Gerard F. Griesser, Trident Mortgage Company LP, Devon, PA; Jim Guy, Microsoft HomeAdvisor, Redmond, WA; Finley Hair, HMS National, Sunrise, FL; Ken Harthausen, HMS National, Sunrise, FL; Rick Hoffman, Coldwell Banker Associates Realty, San Diego, CA; Lawnae Hunter, The Prudential Hunter Realty, Inc., Santa Maria, CA; Karen E. Hupp, RE/MAX Professionals, Sellersburg, IN; Rory J. Johnson, GMAC Home Services, Liberty Corner, NJ; Tom Kemmerer, CBS Home Real Estate Company, Omaha, NE; Kathi King, Harmon Publishing, Dallas, TX; Marcie Knoff, The Personal Marketing Company, Shawnee Mission, KS; William H. Laughlin, C- 21 Laughlin Fine Homes & Estates, McLean, VA; Scott LeForce, Realty World of Northern California & Nevada, Livermore, CA; Ralph A. Leino, Preferred Carlson Realtors, Kalamazoo, MI; John Lomac, San Diego Assn. of Realtors, San Diego, CA; David W. MacIntyre, Arizona Best Real Estate, Scottsdale, AZ; Ron McManamy, Homeland Realty, Sioux City, IA; Jack Meeks, R.E. Professionals of America, Inc., Casselberry, FL; David L. Miller, Cendant Corporation, Parsippany, NJ; David P. Miller, Cavalear Realty Company, Sylvania, OH; Ian Morris, Microsoft HomeAdvisor, Redmond, WA; Mike Napolitano, Dilbeck Realtors BH&G, LaCanada, CA; Bob Nutbrown, Coldwell Banker Pinnacle, Brampton, ON; Pam O'Connor, RELO, Chicago, IL; David C. Paul, Smythe, Cramer Company, Cleveland, OH; John Pembroke, AmeriNet Financial Systems, Inc., Englewood, CO; Patricia J. Petersen, Daniel Gale Real Estate, Huntington, NY; Roy L. Ponthier, First Professional Real Estate School, Inc., Metairie, LA; Dee Premo, Whitehead, Inc. BH&G, Rockford, IL; Richard C. Purvis, RE/MAX of California & Hawaii Inc., Palos Verdes Estates, CA; Alan Pyles, HMS National, Sunrise, FL; Randy Raynolds, Illinois Assn. of Realtors, Springfield, IL; David M. Robbin, Realta, Inc., Northbrook, IL; T. David Rogers, RE/MAX of Eastern Jackson County, Independence, MO; Rita D. Santamaria, Champions School of Real Estate, Houston, TX; Richard L. Schlott, GMAC Home Services, Liberty Corner, NJ; Christopher Schmid, Realty USA, Clifton Park, NY; Dan Schwartz, Dan Schwartz Realty, Inc., Phoenix, AZ; Toni Sherman, Council of Residential Specialists, Chicago, IL; Suzanne Skelly, Coldwell Banker, St. Louis, MO; Bob Slagle, Big Bear Real Estate, Inc., Big Bear Lake, CA; Suzann Slayton, Southern Indiana Realtors Assn., Clarksville, IN; George Slusser, Cendant Corporation, Parsippany, NJ; Almon R. Smith, ARS Consulting, Union, KY; John Stevens, Microsoft HomeAdvisor, Redmond, WA; Stefan Swanepoel, Coldwell Banker Associates Realty, San Diego, CA; Mary Tennant, Keller Williams Realty, Austin, TX; Norm Tesch, Tomlinson Black North, Inc., Spokane, WA; Carol Tintle, Daniel Gale Real Estate, Long Island, NY; Dan Townsend, Keller Williams Realty, San Diego, CA; Vinnie Tracey, RE/MAX International, Inc., Greenwood Village, CO; William G. Vrooman, Nelson Vrooman Associates, Inc., White Plains, NY; Bruce Wallin, Cendant Mobility Broker Network, Parsippany, NJ; Ronald J. Weber, Heartland Multiple Listing Service, Overland Park, KS; Mark T. Wehner, CBS Home Real Estate Company, Omaha, NE; John Wendorff, The Personal Marketing Company, Shawnee Mission, KS; Karin M. Westdale, Westdale BH&G, Grand Rapids, MI; Debby Williams, Big Bear Real Estate, Inc., Big Bear Lake, CA; Mike Zagaris, PMZ Real Estate, Modesto, CA;

Contents

In order to find out where the industry may be going,
it is helpful to understand where we have come from.

Who will be the customers of tomorrow? What will
they want? Who will deliver it? And who will get paid?

If the role of the real estate professional is to survive, it
will do so only for those who are professional counselors;
who know where to get information and how to interpret it;
and who are willing to assume full responsibility for the overall
satisfaction of the consumer, as buyer, seller and homeowner.

Chapter 4:
The Company of the Future   99

Can the erosion of profitability continue? How will the
incursions from Wall Street impact the shape of the
brokerage company? Will the vast majority of business
be concentrated under just a few "brands"? Who will "own"
the customer? And what will be the relationship between
the brokerage firm and its agents?

Chapter 5:
Customer for Life   121

The advent of "one-stop shopping" and concierge
services will expand revenue opportunities and
establish long term relationships. No longer just
"buyers" and "sellers," the homeowner will be a
"customer for life."

Chapter 6:
Niche Marketing   135

Niche marketing concepts will be employed by both
the megabrokers and the mom-and-pop shops.
From first-time buyers to senior citizens, a variety
of niche markets will provide new opportunities
particularly for the techno-savvy agent.

Chapter 7:
The Demise of the Independent Contractor 153

The independent contractor status will come under fire as an
outmoded and extremely inefficient business practice.
New approaches to company profitability will lead to
a variety of alternative compensation structures.

Chapter 8:
The Future of Licensing and Education

Changes in the real estate industry will be reflected
by changes in both licensing laws and real estate education.
Distance learning will supplant much of the on-site training
that has filled the classrooms. Internet delivery of courses
for both pre-licensing and continuing education will
become the norm. Proprietary schools will face intense
competition and form new alliances.

Chapter 9:
The Future of Franchise Organizations

What will be the role of the real estate franchise,
and who will the players be? Will consolidation continue
or will new franchises emerge? Will regional franchises
continue to crop up; and will some of them go national?

Chapter 10:
The Future of Organized Real Estate

What is the future of organized real estate? Will the
associations be capable of adapting to the real estate
world of the future? Will the MLS disappear? And what
effect will that have on association services and membership?
Will the "three-tiered" structure of national, state and
local Realtor associations prevail? Or what will replace it?

Conclusion:
Making the Transition to the Future

Preparing for the unknown and largely unknowable future
will involve developing dynamic strategic plans. While
change is inevitable, the timing and direction of each change
along the way could make the difference between success and
failure. Flexibility and agility will be the hallmarks of the
successful agent and company of the future.

20/20 VISION

A Focus on the Future
of the Real Estate Industry

Charles M. Dahlheimer

Prologue

Ten years ago, we published two books forecasting the direction of the industry during the last decade of the century: *Real Estate in the '90s: A Whole New World Ahead*, and *Coping with the Dynamics of the '90s.*

Going into the twenty-first century, those forecasts have nearly all become history, although a few of them are still in the developmental stages. We predicted that there would be extensive consolidation within the national franchises. (That was long before Cendant appeared on the scene!) We projected a noticeable shrinkage within the ranks of the National Association of Realtors. (There were over 800,000 members then.) We forecasted that representation through buyer agency would become prevalent. (Buyer agency was virtually unheard of then, and the handful of practitioners espousing that concept were considered outside the mainstream of real estate practice.) We suggested that dissension would develop within the ranks of NAR. ("The Alliance" and RIN had not yet been conceived, and Bill Chee's "hungry lion" was just a cub!) We predicted that the local MLS would disappear, and that regional, national and even global listing services would evolve. (The Internet and the World Wide Web would not be introduced to the ordinary consumer until the middle of the decade.) We suggested that the service functions of franchise organizations would change drastically. ("Brand-ing," "strategic alliances" and "one-stop shopping" had not yet become common words in the vocabulary of real estate.) We predicted the expansion of the presence of financial service orga-nizations in the real estate brokerage business--and specifically the fall of the Glass-Steagall Act. (That just happened in No-vember of 1999--but still in time to make our decade deadline!)

As the title "20/20 Vision" suggests, the purpose of this book is to attempt to bring into clear focus the trends and events that will be shaping the real estate industry during the first twenty years of the new millennium.

Why twenty years? Isn't that too far out to seriously plan today, particularly in the light of the rapidity of change that we are experiencing already—not to mention the acceleration of that change as we move forward?

Not really.

Yes, it would be difficult—and a bit presumptuous—to say that our vision goes that far into the future and that we can say with any surety exactly what will transpire over a two-de-cade period of time. But whether you are a broker-owner of a long-established real estate company, an executive officer of one of the major corporations that have just recently ventured into this arena, or a sales associate just embarking on a career in real estate, shouldn't you have some reasonable expectation that this business will still be around in twenty years? . . . and that you are moving into the new millennium on a track that should take you at least twenty years hence—and with some degree of certitude and comfort?

Now that will be possible only if we take a good look at just where this industry is today—and how we got here. And, if we are willing and able to step outside the traditional boundaries of the real estate industry to take a close look at the larger world of commerce in which we are operating—and then apply all that we see there to the smaller world of the real estate buying, selling, investing consumer.

It is only in this way that we can hope to get any kind of clear vision of the future, and any real basis for building a business and/or a career that will have significant future value.

We have also taken the twenty-year approach because so many of the socioeconomic forecasts are based upon trends which have been extended out over that period of time.

Now, we may not be able to say exactly what our industry will look like in the year 2020. But we can say with a great deal of certitude that it will look nothing like the real estate industry in which we are operating today. We cannot put a strict timeline on the changes which we will predict. Some may occur much more quickly than we envision. Others may take longer than expected to materialize. It is safe to say, however, that they will have all occurred, in one fashion or another, by the year 2020. It is also reasonable to assume that none of them will occur overnight. Rather, we will be seeing a gradual transformation rather than a cataclysmic crash.

As important as it is to know what changes might be occurring, it is equally necessary to know something about the timing of those changes.

If one were to read this book and agree with us regarding the structure of the industry that we are predicting, and then decide to totally revise his or her business practices tomorrow, next week or even next year to accommodate all those predictions, the end result would likely be absolute failure.

By the same token, however, those who decide that no change will be needed until some date in the distant future, will find themselves, at best, playing a losing game of "catch up" rather than reaping the profits that this new era will provide.

Strategic planning is the key. This means having an eye on where the industry will eventually be going, and measuring each prospective change in our business practices according to that end view.

For example:

What possible changes might occur in the role of the real estate agent over the next ten years? And how should we begin to adapt our recruiting and hiring practices to accommodate those changes while still meeting the demands of today's marketplace?

Will "one-stop-shopping" become the norm? Then what can we be doing today, tomorrow, to work toward that mode of operation? Or should we decide to differentiate ourselves by focusing on specialty services instead?

Should we maintain our focus on the agent as the true "customer" of the brokerage firm? Or should we strategize to regain direct control of that customer?

And who will our customers be, what will they want, who will deliver it to them and how will they pay for it?

All these questions—and many more—become part of the strategic planning process as we analyze the many changes that may be occurring over just the next few years.

Where there are divergent paths that the industry may follow, successful planning involves the development of strategies that will have validity in a variety of scenarios. Not always easy, granted. But virtually impossible without taking the time to assess the entire landscape.

Some will insist that the industry will continue to change slowly, and that "staying the course" will be sufficient to sail successfully into the future. Some (including the author) see much greater changes coming over the horizon.

To what extent the role of the real estate professional remains central to the real estate transaction may depend in large part upon whether we in the industry are willing to take a proactive role in shaping the industry of the future, or merely sit back and allow our role to be changed—or preempted entirely—because we failed to see the terrain shifting, and perhaps unknowingly and by default, enabled others to seize upon opportunities that should have been ours.

Introduction

The Millennium is not an event. It is a passage—a milestone. After all the reveling, after the Y2K bombs were all defused, New Years Day of the Year 2000 was, after all, just the day after December 31, 1999.

And while it could be argued that the passing of the Millennium is a significant milestone in history, all things are relative.

To the newborn, the dawning of the second day of life marks the beginning of a new twenty-four-hour period which, in itself, will be longer than that infant's entire previous lifespan! At the other extreme, if we accept the scientists' estimate that our universe is more than twelve billion years old, then the turning of a new one-thousand-year period is a rather insignificant event, as there have already been twelve million such events—even though man may have been around to observe and document only a very few of them.

As we look at the many changes that have occurred within the realm of science and technology throughout man's history, it becomes evident that there is a real acceleration factor that takes place as developments in one area tend to impact developments in all areas. The same has been true in the entire world of commerce, and will also apply to the real estate business as the consumer adapts and demands even further changes.

Ben Franklin was already tinkering with electricity in the 1700s, but going into the twentieth century we were still using it for only the very basic purposes of providing light and powering some heavy equipment. It took nearly two hundred years before we discovered that it would do more than just light our way or turn a motor.

In 1876, Alexander Graham Bell filed his patent for the first telephone. (He was nearly beaten to the patent office by Elisha Gray, who had independently developed a very similar invention.) The first permanent outdoor telephone wires were strung in 1877. But an entire century passed before this device broke free of the tether of the hard-wired phone line as cellular communications networks emerged in the mid 1980s. Yet, in just the last few years of the closing decade of the century, much of the technology developed for the cellular world was already becoming obsolete, as the new all-digital networks emerged.

At the beginning of the twentieth century, we were listening to radio signals with primitive devices known as "crystal sets." It was not until the 1950s, with the advent of the transistorized radio, that this communications instrument became truly portable.

In the music industry, recordings were introduced in the late 1800s with the first gramophone. Over the next hundred years, the media on which records were pressed improved, their size was shrunk and the sound quality vastly improved. Tape recording began about mid-century, and it took only twenty years before the cassette revolutionized the way the masses listened to music. Then in just another decade, the Compact Disc was already on its way to making all previous forms of recordings—and playback devices—virtually obsolete.

The first motion pictures hit the screens around the turn of the century. Some seventy-five years later, movies became available for home viewing via the miracle of the home video recorder.

Many industry observers predicted that the advent of the home video player and the video rental business would eventually sound the death knell for the movie theater. Yet theater-going has been steadily increasing. There are more movies being produced today than ever before, due in large part to the expanded revenue streams that video rentals and cable and satellite television have created for the producers.

It should also be noted that while there are more movie theaters today than ever before, they are vastly different from those of just twenty years ago. The survival and growth of the industry was due largely to its ability to adapt to changing consumer needs and to adopt new technology. The single-screen theater has given way to complexes housing a dozen or more mini-theaters, spreading the overhead over a much larger ticket-buying audience, and bringing people back through the doors with much greater frequency, all the while selling them a wide variety of products, from concession stands that look more like cafeterias than the "popcorn counters" of yesteryear—sweatshirts, mugs, toys, videos and CDs all created and licensed by the movie producers as "aftersale" items.

The modern theater also employs state-of-the art technology, providing both a visual and an audio "experience" rivaled only by the most sophisticated home theater installations. It is not just movies they are selling. It is a "total entertainment experience."

Meanwhile, the first electronic computers came on the scene as early as the 1920s, but it took more than half a century longer before microchip technology brought the computer to the desktop, the laptop and the miniaturized notebook.

By way of contrast, the Internet came into being in the early 1970s with the creation of ARPANET—a communications vehicle that connected the scientific community. Twenty years later, the first user-friendly browser was born, bringing the World Wide Web to the masses. Within just the last five years of the twentieth century, the Internet and the World Wide Web introduced the everyday consumer to an entirely new age of communications.

The pace had quickened exponentially!

SO WHAT'S THE POINT?

The point in all this is that it is not just the *inevitability* of change that we need to recognize. We need also to be aware of the *acceleration* of the pace of change. Because any long-term planning will now have to see beyond the technology of the moment—or even of tomorrow—to develop structures that will remain viable, despite ongoing technological changes. And we no longer have the luxury of time that we may have had just a decade ago. In the '80s, real estate boards and associations were focusing much of their attention on getting their MLS data onto the computer and getting agents comfortable with accessing information from the computer rather than from a printed MLS book. It was a bit traumatic, but most of us thought that, once accomplished, we'd be able to ride that wave for quite a long time.

Yes, we saw that the computers would be changing; that newer, faster models would be developed. But I don't think any of us had an inkling of how quickly these relatively expensive new business machines would become obsolete!

Then, just a decade later, we were being warned that the computerized MLS—the very instrument that we had been working so diligently to perfect and to establish as THE tool that would revolutionize the industry—might be the very instrument that would wrest away our control of that industry.

It was in 1993, that NAR president Bill Chee caught the industry's attention by saying that we were like a bunch of Chihuahuas arguing over a bone and unaware that a hungry lion was about to come over the hill.

Concurrently, the information revolution was about to explode with the introduction of the Internet and the World Wide Web to the general public. This was not just a new improvement in computerization, but a total revolution in the world of communications that would not only open up to the consumer market-place a vast amount of information, but would intro-duce a degree of interactivity previously unknown and unimagined.

As far as the future of the MLS—and all the billions of dollars of technology sitting on the desks of our real estate offices and in the homes of our real estate agents—all bets were off! A whole new world was dawning.

THE IMPORTANCE OF FLEXIBILITY

Looking outside the real estate industry, one can find examples of how flexibility has proven to be not only the key to survival, but also the singular attribute that propelled some companies throughout decades of growth and transformation.

Three prominent examples are 3M Corporation, American Express and Microsoft.

3M had its beginnings (and nearly its demise) as a mining venture. The original purpose of the com-pany was to mine a gritty substance known as corun-dum which would then be sold to manufacturers of grinding wheels and sharpening utensils. And while the supply was great, the demand was much lower than its founders had anticipated. To remain in busi-ness, the company decided to move from mining abra-sives to manufacturing abrasive products. They went into the sandpaper business.

Among their customers were automobile paint shops. And the company soon discovered that paint-ers were having problems creating "two tone" paint jobs because there was just no good way to mask off one area while painting the other. This propelled 3M into the manufacturing of masking tape. (Focus on the customer, find a need, and fill it.)

When the company's reputation for producing good masking tape became widespread, it began receiving requests from shippers to create a waterproof shipping tape. This put 3M into the plastic tape business. Its new product, "Scotch Tape," soon became a household word, almost a generic name for plastic tape (right up there with "Frigidaire" for "refrigerator," "Xerox" for copier and oh, yes, "Realtor," for real estate agent or broker!).

Once in the plastic tape business, 3M was poised to lead the charge as the audio recording industry created a demand for magnetized plastic tape. From there, it was a short step to the video recording industry.

Throughout the process, the company discovered that it was not in the mining and manufacturing business at all. It was in the business of problem solving: finding a consumer need and filling it.

American Express started out in the freight express business, and one of the items most frequently requiring express shipments was cash. But in analyzing the movement of cash for commercial transactions, American Express discovered an opportunity for a new product. As merchants in one city were shipping cash to another in payment for goods and material, cash was moving in the other direction as well, for the same reasons. Rather than shipping the cash, the company came to realize that it could just ship vouchers redeemable for cash at the American Express office at the destination end. Merchants could bring their cash to the local express station and vouchers redeemable for cash would be sent to the station at the other end. The cash itself did not have to be moved, but would be used to redeem vouchers shipped in from other stations. Thus the origination of the money order.

Once the company had established this new business, it was a short step to the next product: the traveler's check. The same principles would apply, but for a whole new market.

It was a logical progression from this point to the creation of the company's travel services division.

Meanwhile, the company's previous core businesses were rapidly being eroded by the entry of the U.S. Government into the small package express business (Parcel Post) and the creation of the Postal Money Order. Had the company remained singularly focused on its original objectives and not followed the path of evolutionary progress, it may well have disappeared into oblivion—or, at best, remained just a struggling package express company. (Can't you just see Karl Malden in a truck driver's uniform advising us "Don't ship home without 'em!"?)

Having gradually reinvented itself from shipping into consumer and financial services, this one-hundred-year-old company was well positioned to become one of the leaders in the credit card business in the mid twentieth century, and in a relatively shorter period of time thereafter, into the evolving e-commerce revolution.

Microsoft Corporation was founded in 1975. Twenty years later, founder and CEO Bill Gates expressed the company's mission statement as "a computer on every desk, in every home." Just four years later, reading the progress of the Internet and Internet-based applications, the company had the boldness to announce that its vision had shifted. Microsoft was now looking beyond the PC and recognizing the emerging importance of central servers. In July, 1999, a new mission statement recognizing Internet-based software and services, non-PC services, hand-held computers and TV set boxes, was enunciated by company president Steve Ballmer: "Empower people through great software, anytime, any place and on any device."

The company that had just about written the rules for the computer industry was now guaranteeing itself a position in the future by not holding too fast to its successes of the past. The expanding world of the central server would now become the expanded world of Microsoft products and services.

In all three examples, 3M, American Express and Microsoft, note the power of vision—and the empowerment of flexibility!

EMPOWERMENT

In the future, our planning will not only have to incorporate the various iterations in technology, but will have to go far beyond that, taking into consideration the many variables that influence consumer demand and consumer accessibility to both information and service.

High tech and high touch will both remain important, and the profitable integration of the two will be a major key to success for both companies and agents moving into the new millennium.

No one can predict exactly what the real estate industry will look like at any given point along that timeline. One thing is certain, however: It is moving into vast new unexplored territories. And it is not necessarily moving on its own volition. It is being rushed along by the pace of the world around it.

It is also a certainty that those who feel they can continue doing what they have been doing, without making a series of timed, serious adjustments— and who persist in that feeling despite numerous warnings to the contrary—will probably not be around the industry by the time we reach 2020.

Similarly, those who, seeing the changes that will be taking place in the future, abandon their current practices to implement an entirely new model, will also be in great jeopardy, as changes require a certain amount of time before they can be assimilated. Throughout recorded history, many an inventor has starved, many an innovator been banished and many a revolutionary shot—simply because they were ahead of their times.

The challenge for the real estate broker and agent will be not only to stay ahead of the curve, but to do so without alienating oneself and one's business practices from the landscape of the present. However, we are not talking about "gradual" change, or about adapting to the way others have changed around us. That's re-active, and it's a pattern for failure—and all the more so as changes begin occurring more rapidly.

It takes great vision and flexibility and a keen sense of timing to navigate the winds of change without steering too far off course.

This book was written just at the turn of the

new millennium. Those who pick it up at some point along the continuum between the turn of the millennium and the year 2020 will find that some of the events that we are predicting will have already occurred. Others may seem a lot more likely to occur once certain other events have taken place.

And, if our projections are correct, at some point along that timeline this book will become utterly obsolete as a strategic planning guide (but its relevance as a history book will endure!). But wouldn't it be nice to be able to have that vision in advance—to be able to evaluate each trend in its true light—as either an emerging opportunity or a siren song that will call the unsuspecting to shipwreck on the rocks of change?

As you make your way through this book, you will no doubt find a number of scenarios that seem a bit unrealistic or implausible, but only when evaluated solely by the criteria of the past or the present—criteria which will be constantly evolving in the future.

Consider, for example, these scenarios: When we predict that the independent contractor status (as we now know it) will all but disappear, being supplanted by an all-employee framework...Or when we predict that the "single licensing" concept will lead the way to LLPs or LLCs whose principals will all be independent brokers...Or when we talk about "career pathing"—a system that provides a track on which the would-be real estate career professional moves from rank neophyte all the way through to seasoned professional with specialized knowledge and experience—and, more than likely, ownership in the firm in which he or she has learned the trade.

All of these things may seem a bit far-fetched right now, and inconsistent with existing business practices. But the future may well be inconsistent with existing business practices. Considered in the light of the rapidly changing world of commerce and communications in which we are already living, these future scenarios might appear much more plausible.

And (this is very important) every trend that we examine must be evaluated not in isolation, but in conjunction with all the rest of the emerging trends which we are able to identify. There will be a synergistic effect—each change helping to pave the way for all the others, as the chaos of the twenty-first century unfolds!

There are those who feel that the real estate industry will keep pretty much on track, with a steady pace of evolution.

Yes, there will be some shrinking in the ranks, they say, but probably no more than ten to twenty percent. And, after all, this has already been anticipated for nearly ten years. As in the past, they reason, the big will continue to get bigger. But there will always be room for the smaller, well-managed shop. Niche marketers will continue to succeed.

They concede that there will be some consumers who want to pay for only certain of the services traditionally associated with listing and selling, and do the rest themselves. But they feel that the majority will still want the real estate agent to handle the entire transaction.

They readily concede that there will continue to be intense bottom-line pressure, and brokerage firms will probably have to adjust the commission splits in

order to stay in business. But they feel that top producing agents will continue to build their "company
within the company," and get the lion's share of the
commission, which necessitates the continuation of
"revolving door" recruiting.

And while they agree that the trend toward more
highly educated, career-oriented recruits will continue,
they also contend that for the most part, new agents
will continue to come into the business in much the
same fashion and for most of the same reasons as before, being attracted to the entrepreneurial nature of
the business or seeking to augment their family income with some real estate commissions.

While there is a chance that things may play
out this way, we are more inclined to believe that not
only will the pace of change quicken, but the depth
and extent of the changes will be much more profound,
altering the entire structure of the industry—perhaps
altogether eliminating the industry as we know it.

Don't get me wrong. People will continue to buy
and sell homes—and to need all the services traditionally associated with the process—and, in fact, probably even more services. But whom they will go to for
those services, how those services will be provided and
how they will be paid for may all be in the balance
right now.

In this book, we will attempt to progress from
the known to the unknown; from where the industry
is today, and how it got there, to where it will be during the opening decades of the twenty-first century.

We will be presenting some scenarios that may
seem a bit far-fetched. For those readers who have
been around the real estate industry for some time,

and particularly those who have built very successful companies and careers in the real estate industry, the challenge will be much more difficult than it will for those who are relative newcomers and who are not mesmerized by remembrances of "the way we were." It is hard to break old traditions, old habits, paradigms—hard to think "outside the box" when we have spent our lives building that box!

The real challenge will be neither to simply accept the scenarios that we portray here nor to build convincing arguments against them. Rather, the challenge will be to think through these scenarios with a "What If" mentality. For example:

Perhaps you currently have three offices and 120 salespeople, all on various commission splits. What if the trend moves to salaried agents? Could you safely (and profitably) segue into the salaried mode using your existing sales staff? How should the possibility of that occurring influence your current recruiting and training?

What if you begin gearing up for that and it does not become a reality within the industry? Will you have gone beyond the point of turning back? Or will the salaried mode be viable for you even though it has not been generally adopted by the industry? Should you continue in that direction and build a niche around that very difference?

Should you reevaluate your current methods of recruiting, hiring and training and establish standards that will prove successful whether that transition occurs or not?

Are there changes that the salaried structure would force you to make that should actually be made even under your current compensation structure? And how would those changes impact both agent and company bottom-line profitability?"

Those are the kinds of questions we hope these chapters will inspire.

Be forewarned, however, that we cannot presume to provide definitive answers. Successful long-range planning involves knowing what questions to ask, analyzing a variety of potential pitfalls and opportunities, and developing strategies that are fluid, not cast in stone.

Flexibility is paramount. The ability to keep an open mind and a willingness to ask "What if this happens?" rather than to decree "This will not happen!" will distinguish the successful planners from the business flare-outs of the future.

Chapter 1:

The Perspectives of History

In order to get some perspective on where the real estate industry is headed, it is helpful to understand some of the historical developments that have taken place in the industry during recent decades.

While some would say that the real estate business goes back to the earliest recorded history—as long as man has had a sense of property ownership—the real estate *brokerage* business as we know it today is a relative newcomer on the historical scene.

And, prior to the last few decades of the twentieth century, the brokerage business remained relatively unchanged.

The real estate business during the '60s, for example, looked very much like the real estate business at the turn of the twentieth century. Individuals who were "brokers" worked with clients who were either wanting to sell a house or buy a house. If they had a seller, they would search for a buyer. Once found, they would attempt to bring the two together to complete a transaction. If they had the buyer, they would canvass for someone wanting to sell the kind of house their buyer was looking for.

This was pretty much the same scenario in both the commercial and residential arenas.

Once agreement was reached, the buyer would go to his bank or building and loan company to finance the purchase. Frequently, the seller would take back a deed of trust, or private lenders or mortgage bankers would provide the financing.

The loan was often an "interest only" note, with a balloon repayment due after a period of time—often just five years. It was not uncommon for the borrower to be able to pay only the interest—usually due quarterly—and when the note matured, perhaps pay off a portion of the principal and renew the balance for another period. Amortized loans with monthly principal and interest payments did not become commonplace until the second half of the century.

There was no MLS, and often not even a formal "listing" as we know it today. If a broker had a contact that brought him in touch with someone wanting to sell, he would take the information, work out a commission agreement (sometimes in writing) and quietly look for a matching buyer. If another broker had a buyer and happened to locate that same seller, he would do the deal and get the commission. The co-brokerage concept only took hold during the last half of the century.

While the MLS concept had its beginnings in the late '40s, well into the '60s there were still many locations around the nation that had not yet fully embraced the concept.

So, for at least the first half of the twentieth century, there was very little change in the industry or in the way the residential real estate business was transacted. The real estate brokerage business at the opening of the decade of the '60s looked for all intents and purposes very much the same as it did at the beginning of the century.

NEW BUSINESS STRUCTURES

The '60s could be called "The Era of the Referral," as the real estate industry awakened to new opportunities with the dawning of the age of corporate relocation. Within the first three years of that decade, three major national referral networks came into existence: RELO (then called Inter-City Relocation, and still in existence today); All Points (which merged with RELO in the '90s); and National Multi List Service (later to be known as the Homes For Living Network).

Real estate companies that once served only a very small number of local communities were now becoming involved with transactions thousands of miles away and, in the process, were beginning to communicate with companies in a variety of different communities. Not only were customers and commissions shared, but so also were ideas. New business models began to emerge, focused specifically on capturing relocation business.

ENTER THE FRANCHISES
AND CORPORATE GIANTS

The '70s marked the beginning of franchising in the real estate industry and the advent of the 100 percent commission structure. While both concepts had a dramatic effect on the internal structure of the industry, from the consumer's viewpoint, little had changed. The franchises created national "brands" and all the advertising and hype that goes along with them. However the relationship between the real estate company and the customer, and the way real estate services were delivered to that customer remained virtually unchanged.

Transitioning into the '80s, the first "corporate giants" entered the residential real estate arena. Merrill Lynch, Pearce, Fenner and Smith made its first acquisition in 1979, the Paula Stringer Company of Dallas. Merrill's plans were to buy out or buy into forty of the nation's leading residential brokerage firms "as a natural expansion of its business en route to becoming an overall financial center."

In 1981, Sears, Roebuck & Company decided to reformat its business mission, electing to expand into the full realm of financial services. In one single week in 1981, Sears added Dean Witter Securities to its holdings and bought Coldwell Banker Real Estate.

Both new players saw real estate as a natural adjunct to the financial services business. However, neither company was very successful at realizing any synergies between its existing customer base and that of its real estate acquisitions.

Both stayed in the real estate business for about ten years, with Merrill selling to Prudential in 1989 and Sears selling to the Freemont Group in 1992.

Meanwhile, in 1985, Metropolitan Life jumped on the "synergy-seeking" bandwagon with the acquisition of Century 21 from TransWorld.

No one can question the lasting impact that was created by the entrance of such major national giants into an industry that had previously been extremely provincial in ownership and outlook. However, much as with the advent of franchising, there were really no substantive changes in the end product from the buyer's or seller's viewpoints. Nor did the day-to-day business of listing and selling change, with the exception, perhaps, of the percentage of the commission raked off the top to cover franchise fees.

A NEW ERA DAWNS

In the mid '90s, three trends developed that would set the stage for a dramatic revolution—and one that would leave the real estate industry forever changed. And, significantly, all three had a common focus: the consumer.

1. Consumer Representation

First came the focus on agency representation. While creating a lot of furor in the mid '90s, the significance of the buyer agency movement is not so much in its direct impact on the delivery of real estate services (although some distinct changes did evolve), as in the fact that its impetus came from outside the industry itself. The brokerage industry did not create buyer agency. It did not adopt buyer agency because it wanted to—or even because it made more sense. Buyer agency was forced upon the industry as a response to consumer demands.

And the extent to which the industry changed as a result was testimony to the fact that we had indeed entered an era where the consumer would be king.

2. Non-Real-Estate Players Take on Real Estate as a Core Business

The second trend was the incursion of certain non-real-estate entities into real estate as a core business. Indirectly, this was also the result of a new focus on the consumer. The focus of the real estate business would no longer be on the real estate transaction—a series of isolated incidents involving "listings" and "sales." The business would now be centered on the consumer as "homeowner," who is sometimes the buyer, sometimes the seller, but always the customer for a multitude of products and services. The customer would become the core around which the business would be reinvented. And access to that customer would be considered the heart and soul of the business.

The new trend began to take shape in 1995, when a company previously unknown to the real estate industry began its foray into the real estate franchise arena. Hospitality Franchise Systems, Inc. (HFS) acquired Century 21, and proclaimed that it would "write the rules for real estate." By the middle of 1996, the company had also acquired ERA Franchise Systems and Coldwell Banker.

In the following year, HFS would announce its merger with CUC, a massive direct marketing enterprise. (The combined companies eventually would be renamed "Cendant" in 1998.)

In addition to its real estate franchise systems, HFS was also a direct owner and operator of real estate companies through its National Realty Trust, a unit first established to hold and manage the Coldwell Banker owned-and-operated offices. In 1997, HFS formed a joint venture with Apollo Management, LP, to create a new entity, NRT, which would not only own those existing companies, but would serve as an acquisition arm, feeding new companies into each of the HFS brand franchises. By 1998, NRT had become the nation's largest real estate company with 692 offices and more than $84 billion in sales volume.

Nineteen ninety-eight also saw General Motors get into the real estate arena with the acquisition of Better Homes & Gardens by its GMAC unit. Intent on bolstering its presence in key market areas, GMAC would also launch its own acquisition program. Companies thus acquired would operate under the "GMAC Real Estate" banner and the existing franchises would eventually be changed over, as the name "Better Homes & Gardens" was not part of the sale to GMAC. By separate agreements, Meredith Corporation would allow GMAC the use of the name for a ten-year period following the sale.

MidAmerican Energy Holdings, an Iowa-based gas and electric energy company, also entered the arena in 1998 and by year's end had become the nation's second-largest residential brokerage company.

In addition to its core utility business, MidAmerican announced its intentions to transform itself into a major consumer services company, with real estate leading the charge.

In the fall of 1999, an investor group led by Warren Buffett's legendary Berkshire Hathaway, Inc. announced that it had reached a definitive agreement to acquire MidAmerican Energy Holding Company. Meanwhile, its real estate subsidiary closed its Initial Public Offering and began operations as HomeServices.Com, Inc. Its business objective is "to become a seamless provider of a comprehensive menu of products and services for the total homeownership experience, particularly by means of e-commerce." Its growth strategy includes the cross-selling of real estate-related products and services, including mortgage, title and insurance.

Unlike the acquisitions of the '80s which saw the acquired real estate entities as adjuncts to the companies' core businesses, the business models that had evolved in the '90s envision real estate operations as core business units.

Wall Street had come to Main Street—and the real estate industry would be forever changed.

3. The Advent of E-Commerce

The third event promises to have a profound impact not only on the world of real estate, but on virtually every form of commerce worldwide: the advent of the Internet and the e-commerce revolution.

The developments in information and communications technology that occurred during just the last decade of the twentieth century are propelling us not only into the new millennium—but into a whole new world where business, finance, education, life-style, entertainment—you name it—virtually nothing will remain untouched or unchanged.

We are just at the beginning of the e-commerce revolution, and most real estate practitioners are having some difficulty understanding where all this may be taking them—and the industry with which they have grown accustomed.

Some are still in a state of denial, thinking that we'll keep on going with a little change here, a little adjustment there. Others have accepted the reality, but haven't a clue where it is all going.

Hindsight usually proves much better than foresight. How much easier it would be to plan for the future if we could magically jump forward in time to the year 2020 and see how the events of the next twenty years will play out.

We can't do that, of course. But we can look back in time to see how the real estate industry reacted to other challenges and opportunities, and, perhaps use lessons from the past to help shape our thinking about the future.

AN ERA OF MISSED OPPORTUNITIES

One of the most dramatic lessons from the past comes out of the world of corporate relocation.

Although the events of the '60s and '70s were not as dramatic as those lightning-fast changes that propelled us into the new millennium, they are perhaps the most enlightening, because we can now view them from the clearer perspective that only time can provide. The real estate industry's reaction to the developments in the relocation marketplace provide a rather telling story for those who are willing to take the time to sort it all out. It is a story about what can happen when we lose our focus—a story of missed opportunities.

Consider the fact that just forty years ago, at the beginning of the decade of the '60s, real estate was an extremely provincial business. The typical company had one office and perhaps a half dozen or dozen licensees. A company with two or three offices would have been a "megabroker" (although that term had not yet been coined.) There were no referral networks of any kind. The franchise concept was not yet even a dream. There was no ownership of real estate companies by any national concerns.

And this is much the way it had been throughout the history of the industry.

But all this would change—and change radically—within just the next few years, leaving an imprint on the industry that would lay the groundwork for even more monumental changes during the remaining years of the century.

It is precisely how we looked at those changes as they came about—and particularly the blindness that seemed to plague traditional practitioners—that presents a lesson that should encourage us to take a more proactive approach to where our industry is going over the next two decades.

With the advent of corporate relocation, some of the basic needs of the customer—be it the buyer or the seller—underwent radical change. A new residential "customer," the corporate employer, emerged, bringing with it a source of "bulk" business for those who pursued relocation seriously.

The relocating sellers were no longer moving into a larger house in the neighborhood, or perhaps out to the new suburban subdivisions, where their local agent could assist them with (and earn a commission from) both ends of the transaction. Now they were moving across the country, to areas totally unknown to them— and to their agent.

Some system needed to be developed to handle the transferee's needs at the homefinding side of the relocation—as well as a method by which the listing agent back home could somehow make a commission off that next sale—albeit a thousand miles away. The concept of the "referral network" cropped up as the answer to both those needs.

During the opening several years of the '60s, the first two real estate referral networks came into existence. Leading the way was a not-for-profit organization known (even to this day) as "RELO." It was to be an organization of independent brokerage firms who would agree to cooperate on relocations and share fees on a referral basis.

Hot on RELO's heels was an organization that called itself the "National Multi List Service" (NMLS). While both were focused on relocation, NMLS provided a unique twist to the concept: NMLS published a monthly magazine entitled "Homes For Living" for each of its members, featuring pictures, prices and descriptions of homes currently for sale in the member's area. These magazines were then distributed monthly throughout the NMLS network, so that

each member office featured a display of magazines
from all other members, providing a pictorial "national
MLS" to help transferees learn about property and
neighborhoods in the destination location—and to help
lock those transferees in to working with the NMLS
member in the destination city.

(To keep things in perspective, remember that
there were no "Homes" magazines or other property
marketing brochures in circulation in the marketplace
at that time. Classified ads, *sans* pictures, in local
newspapers were virtually the only real estate information resource that consumers had, other than con-
tacting a real estate agent and asking about property.)

Before the end of the next decade, more than
fifty referral networks would appear on the scene, each
with its own unique twist, and each offering certain
more or less proprietary products and services to assist its members in capturing relocation business.

So the industry began to respond to this new
demand and to learn to tap profitably into the new
opportunities that relocation would afford.

However, the traditional referral network ad-
dressed only one side of the relocation equation: helping the transferee at the destination end. But problems were looming on the other side of the equation:
While the homefinding process in the destination city
was becoming a bit easier, getting the employees' existing homes sold at the origin end of the move was
becoming one of the major issues.

Some brokerage firms, usually the larger and
better-established ones, created a concept called the
"Guaranteed Sales Plan" as a means of assuring that
the transferee would have his equity in time to close

on the home in the new location. On the surface, the GSP sounded like a reasonable plan. "List your home with us. If it doesn't sell within the sixty (or ninety, or whatever) days provided by your employer, we'll buy it. Simple as that." But, while sounding reasonable at first blush, the concept was fraught with problems.

First of all, in order to make the offer, the brokerage firm had to be assured that the home could be purchased at a price that would allow it to at least break even should the home remain on the market for several months following its acquisition. This meant that the "buy-out offer" extended to the transferee would have to be a "lowball" offer—one not often seen as very desirable by the outgoing transferee.

Then, there was the problem of having cash available to do the deal when a home did not sell during the listing period. Most brokers handled this by establishing a line of credit at their local bank to provide whatever cash might be needed to cover at least the equity interest of the transferees.

An even larger problem was the fact that the transferee generally was not very happy with the "lowball" buyout offer. And when the transferee isn't happy, the corporate employer isn't happy. That's just a fact of life in the relocation industry. And when the customer is not happy, that's a cue for someone else who is waiting in the wings!

THE THIRD-PARTY REVOLUTION

Enter a new service industry: The relocation management or "third-party" company.

When one compares the methodology of the

third-party company with that of the real estate industry there are a number of very important lessons to be learned.

Most important, the relocation management industry focused on the problem of getting the transferee's home sold and saw it as the corporate employer's problem. And, based on this observation, they developed a solution that would work—but whose costs would be born by the corporation. (If it's the corporate employer's problem, they reasoned, then the corporate employer will pay for the solution.)

In the relocation management scenario, the problems involved with getting the transferee's home sold would be taken off the shoulders of both the transferee and the corporate employer. The transferee would get a fair value for the home, with the buyout offer based on the average of two or more independent appraisals. Further, the money needed for the buyout would be advanced by the third-party company, but as an interest-bearing loan to the corporate employer.

All of the work involved in the home purchase and resale scenario would be either performed by the third-party company—for a fee—or would be contracted out to others by the third-party company and then billed back to the corporate employer, along with an additional management fee.

If the home had to be purchased and resold, all of the expenses relating to the process were billed back to the employer, along with a management fee. And if the home sold at a loss, the loss would be borne by the corporate employer.

The relocation was the problem of the corporate employer. The solution was provided, at a fee, by the relocation management company.

From the mid '60s through the mid '80s, third-party companies increased their hold on the relocation marketplace.

Meanwhile, the real estate community began to take a new look at relocation: Since a large percentage of relocation business was being concentrated in the hands of the third-party companies, those real estate practitioners who were serious about developing this business made an all-out effort to court the relocation management companies. They saw this as their entree to a stream of business, focusing their efforts quite narrowly on getting these third-party listings.

But in so doing they once again took their eye off the ball. While they should have been studying the real needs of the corporate customer, they were mesmerized by the siren song of third-party listings and left the door wide open for yet another industry to appear on the scene to eat the Realtor's lunch!

With an increasing percentage of corporate transferee's homes going into the buyout mode, and with escalating costs of carrying and marketing that inventory of homes, the cost of the average relocation had climbed through the $40,000 mark by the mid '80s. At the same time, corporations were beginning to feel the bottom-line pinch and hearing the growing demand for fiscal restraints and shareholder value.

A study done in the mid '80s showed that when a transferee's home was sold during the initial listing period and did not have to go into the buyout process, the total cost of that relocation was approximately half the cost of a similar relocation in which the transferee's home had to be purchased and then resold.

There was a clear message in this, but the real estate practitioners just weren't hearing it: Instead of courting the relocation management companies to get hold of the listings, the real estate industry should have been presenting their corporate customers with a program that would get more of those homes sold before the transferee's deadline.

(Identify the customer's real problem, find a workable solution, and the customer will pay for it.)

And who would have been better positioned to provide such a program than the real estate companies who would ultimately be responsible for the success of the home-selling process?

Again, the solution came from outside the real estate industry.

ENTER "ADVANCE MARKETING"

As with the advent of the third-party relocation industry, the Advance Marketing company was able to identify the specific problem that the corporate employers were having and provide a solution. And, as with the third-party industry, the Advance Marketers would be paid handsomely for the solution.

The solution put forward by the Advance Marketing companies was to create a stronger partnership between the corporate employee and the employer in the effort to get the home sold early on. This would be done by counseling with the transferee before the home was listed to help the transferee better understand the home sale process—and the role that pricing has to play in that process.

Then, the Advance Marketers would select specific real estate agents within the seller-transferee's marketplace who had an A-Plus track record on getting homes sold within the transferee's specific neighborhood. Those agents would then be given a detailed marketing plan and be held accountable for periodic progress reports, scheduled reviews with the seller, and a variety of incentives and strategies to help drive the selling process.

Advance Marketers also convinced the corporate employers that additional bonuses for getting the home sold early in the listing period would be cost-effective tools for enlisting the cooperation of both the seller-transferee and the agents within the marketplace.

In other words, the program put forth by the Advance Marketing industry was just good old common sense listing practice! And, interestingly enough, the people who made the Advance Marketing programs work were none other than the real estate agents who got those listings!

But who got paid? You guessed it! Not the real estate practitioners. They got their usual commission (at least until the third-party players realized that this business could command some hefty referral fees!). But, like the third-party companies, the Advance Marketing folks charged the corporate employers a separate fee (often in the area of $1,200 to $1,500 per transferee) for taking on the management of each transferee's home sale process! And this was not unreasonable. The corporate employers had a severe problem—and it was getting worse each year. Advance Marketing helped turn that around, and the corporate employer was more than happy to pay the fee.

There is no doubt that many individual real estate agents had been providing similar services all along—and without charging an additional fee. What Advance Marketing gurus brought to the picture was consistency, methods and systems to guarantee results. Most importantly, they brought the corporate employer into the solution, tailoring relocation policies that encouraged and rewarded employee cooperation. They did not rely on the individual real estate agent to do a good job. They established marketing programs that had to be followed, and reporting systems to make sure they were being implemented.

The point in all this is that the real estate industry itself should have had the insight and taken the initiative to create a similar program—and, as a result, reap similar rewards.

The lesson for the real estate practitioner is to be careful not to get dragged off course. Don't narrow your focus to see only what others in the industry around you are doing. Rather, get your focus on the customer's real needs. Look for ways to bring new solutions to the table. Think "outside the box." Don't hesitate to look outside traditional "real estate" and even to look to other industries for guidelines and possibly even partnerships in developing programs and services that will be right on target.

If the solutions are viable, they don't have to be given away. They can be sold. But they have to work! The customer must come out better, even after paying a fee for the solution. That's a win-win.

Throughout this book we will continually draw the focus away from "business as usual" and to refocus on the real needs of the consumer. Because the consumer is the key to the future.

Chapter 2:

The Consumer of Tomorrow

A lot has been said about keeping the Realtor at the center of the transaction.

While that is definitely an issue about which all of us in this business should legitimately be concerned, the focus is just a bit misdirected. In order to remain essential to the transaction, and especially to the "total experience" of the transaction, the real estate industry needs to reposition itself as the singular driving force that will assure that the *consumer* remains at the center of the transaction, and that the entire home-ownership experience is viewed as profitable and rewarding largely because of the care and attention provided by the real estate professional.

In preparing a game plan for the next twenty years, we should want to know who the consumer of tomorrow will be and what services he or she will require. Equally important, we need to analyze what relationships the real estate company and agent will have with that consumer, how they will be established, nurtured and maintained and, ultimately, how those relationships will be turned into bottom-line profit.

Unfortunately, most broker-owners and agents today would have a difficult time getting their hands around who the consumer of *today* is. Few of the real estate practitioners operating at the local level have either the training or the inclination to be very analytical about such things as demographics and market trends.

Sure, we know something about how our ads are pulling, which media seem to be the most productive, whether the phone rings more from our yard signs than from our newspaper ads. We may even know what types of direct marketing seem to be getting the best response.

But, for the most part, we don't really know why. What is it about the consumer today that drives them toward our company or our agent? What might be pulling them away?

Equally important, how is the consumer changing—and, more specifically, what else is happening that may influence the consumer's approach to the home purchase and sale processes tomorrow?

We have all asked those questions, and sometimes we have come up with reasonable and workable answers.

But now let's ask the question not with relationship to just our own company, but rather to the entire industry in which we are engaged: What is it about the consumer of today that drives them toward any real estate company or agent? What pulls them away? And, what is changing that may pull them closer to us or banish us entirely from their list of service vendors?

MOVE TOWARD SELF-DETERMINATION

During the closing two decades of the twentieth century, we saw definite movement toward self-determination on the part of the consumer. But sometimes it is hard to tell what is the cause and what the effect. In the retail merchandising industry, did the large superstores crop up because the consumer wanted them? Or did the consumer learn to like the self-determination that the warehouse store offered only after such institutions came into existence? Was there a loud cry from the consumer marketplace denouncing the mom-and-pop store and demanding the creation of the superstore? Or did very savvy marketers understand that "if we build it, they will come"?

At one time, the retailing pundits said that there may be a certain segment of the population that would take to the "discount" store concept, but that a sizable segment—particularly the more affluent and more educated—would remain faithful to the more customer-focused specialty shops because the best brands would always be found there and because of the personal attention that would not be available at the mass merchandisers.

It didn't take very long, however, for that prediction to be proven false. The assumptions upon which it had been based were false. Producers of name brands will place them wherever they can best reach the marketplace. And consumers are interested in convenience, but not necessarily personal service. And they will go wherever they can get the best deal on the best brands in the most convenient fashion. The best brands began to show up on the mass merchandisers' shelves. The superstore provided an opportunity for the discriminating shopper to examine a wide variety of products, from a host of manufacturers, all available to see and touch and sample—all under the same roof and at very competitive prices.

Industry analysts have estimated that one hundred million shoppers pass through the doors of Wal-Mart and Sam's Club each week. A very impressive figure, considering that the total population of the United States is only two hundred seventy million and there are only seventy million family households. (Another very impressive figure is that approximately one in every three hundred Americans is an employee of this merchandising giant. If it sold only to its own employees and their families, it could maintain a fairly sizable market share!)

It is also interesting to note that back in the '50s, Sam Walton had just lost his lease and moved to Bentonville, Arkansas, to start a new five-and-dime store. In the ensuing thirty to forty years, most of Walton's compatriots—the small five-and-dime owners—went out of business, bowing to the pressures of the marketplace, most of which were being created by the large discounters and mass merchandisers.

The mass merchandisers have moved closer to the consumer, using pricing, store hours and brand-name availability to woo even the most discerning shopper.

Meanwhile, unable to compete with the giants,

and disappointed and distressed at the lack of customer loyalty, many mom and pop stores closed their doors. Many of the upscale merchandisers also changed their tactics to compete, often reducing the amount of sales personnel on the floor. They had discovered that one of the specific attractions of the warehouse stores was that customers could do all the "just looking" they wanted, without being disturbed or coerced by a salesperson. What had once been perceived as a customer benefit—and a rather expensive one, from the merchandiser's point of view—was now viewed by consumers in a more negative fashion as a way for the store to "get their claws into you" and push you either into a sale or out the door.

And manufacturers catered to the needs of the mass merchandisers, with pricing often below that previously available to the distributors, and sometimes with specific models available exclusively through the mass merchandisers. The mass merchandisers proved that they could attract the customers, and the manufacturers lined up, vying for shelf space.

The consumer had changed—partly by choice, but partly by design of the merchandising geniuses. And the entire marketplace was falling in line, from manufacturers to competitive retailers to the consumers themselves—in order to catch the wave!

At the turn of the millennium, the mass merchandisers look warily over their shoulder at the burgeoning e-commerce marketplace, where massive price wars are developing. The playing field is far from level, as these cyberstore operations avoid a great many of the expenses traditionally related to displaying product and servicing the walk-in shopper. No expensive mall leases, no salaries for personnel to stock the shelves, no more losses due to shoplifting, no more damaged or shelf-worn merchandise due to careless handling by marauding consumers! And they are reaching the public with an advertising medium that is essentially free!

Take, for example, the remarkable success of Amazon.com, the overnight giant in the world of book-sellers. A boon, no doubt, for the package delivery industry, but a threat to the very existence of the traditional book retailer—unless, of course, these aging giants can come up with features, advantages and benefits of their way of doing business that will overcome the lure of the e-commerce transaction.

More likely, however, there will be a merger of the two industries, with e-commerce giants owning strategically placed warehouse stores, (or the warehousing giants owning e-commerce sites) with some inventory going off the shelf and through the checkout lanes and even more going out the back door to e-commerce shoppers. The superstore could become the hands-on showroom, capturing both the customer who has not learned to go shopping electronically and those who want to see and touch a specific product before purchasing.

And then there's Ebay, the Internet site that offers consumers the opportunity to bid for all kinds of merchandise on an auction basis. Upon its launch, the site was an immediate success. However, the company discovered that people wanting to buy or sell large, bulky items were not able to deal effectively with the site, as shipping and delivery problems and expenses were an inherent problem with a national auction site.

To solve the problem, and to greatly expand EBay's marketplace throughout the nation, the company experimented with a local site, called EBayLA to provide a site on which Los Angeles area consumers could buy and sell goods for delivery within the local marketplace. Local area bidders swarmed the site, purchasing items such as automobiles, furniture and appliances.

Having created a viable local model, EBay is now opening fifty distinct local Internet sites targeted at the largest metropolitan areas nationwide. (Keep an eye on the customer!)

THE MODEL FOR REAL ESTATE

Will the consumer take to "one-stop shopping" in the real estate transaction? Many have pointed to failed past attempts to link other products and services with the real estate company and agent at the center of the transaction.

During the past two decades, there were numerous attempts to get real estate agents to hawk all sorts of other products, some more directly related to the real estate transaction, such us insurance and warranties and mortgage products. Others seemed less fitting, such as home remodeling services, replacement windows and siding, alarm systems, lawn services and the like.

It was thought that the real estate agent would refer clients to these ancillary businesses if the agent could realize some piece of change from each referred transaction. However, compared with the real estate commission earned on each transaction, the incremental amount that would be passed on to the agent as a result of such referred business seemed too insignificant to persuade most successful agents to become "hucksters" in the eyes of their valued clientele.

Many agents considered themselves above involvement with the sales of household products and services, feeling that this would demean their professionalism in the eyes of the consumer. A great many more just didn't think there would be sufficient revenue stream from such activities to be worth the additional effort.

But today's affinity marketing programs are not agent-driven. In fact, the one-stop shopping that is being envisioned for the future may even put many real estate agents out of business—at least the traditional agents, operating as independent contractors and earning the lion's share of commission dollars.

And the key will be control of the customer.

If the mass marketers of the real estate industry can gain control of the customer through affinity programs that provide turn-key services, true one-stop shopping and discount pricing on all the elements of the real estate transaction, then the customers will come to them—just as they did to the mass retail merchandisers. And the role of the real estate agent will be greatly diminished.

All this has nothing to do with how we, the real estate practitioners, want things to go. Nor does it even have much to do with how the consumer of today envisions the real estate transaction to be structured. It has everything to do with how Big Business interests can combine to create a whole new way of doing business—one in which the consumer's needs are met, and sometimes even surpassed, and profit margins literally soar, compared with the meager profits that the real estate brokerage industry has come to accept.

THE CONSUMER DOES NOT WANT TO BE IN THE REAL ESTATE BUSINESS

It is important that we keep in mind the fact that the average consumer is not in the business of buying and selling homes. For the typical consumer, a real estate transaction may occur every five to seven years. This should be taken into consideration when studying and applying some of the information that can be gleaned from marketing surveys and consumer research studies.

One of the secrets to the success of the mass merchandiser is the convenience which the large "everything-under-one-roof" store provides. People dislike having to go from store to store to purchase the items on their shopping list. They prefer to get everything in one place, provided the quality and the price is competitive.

And the mass merchandiser has another advantage. While customers may come to the store looking for a specific product, they pass through aisles loaded with other products—often very alluringly displayed—and frequently end up with many more items in the shopping cart than they had originally planned. A trip to Home Depot for a new garden hose could trigger the sale of a new lawn mower or a gas grille. Or it may trigger the remodeling of a kitchen or bath or the addition of a deck, spa or swimming pool!

So how do we translate all that into our real
estate business?

- First, we need to take seriously the business of
  learning as much as we can about our customers—present, past and future—and about the
  demographics, culture and buying habits of the
  residents of the communities in which we operate.
- Second, we have to determine just what services
  can be packaged together into a true one-stop
  shopping experience.
- Third, we have to make certain that our clients
  and customers have a truly satisfying experience in every contact with our company.
- Fourth, we need to look beyond the real estate
  transaction itself—and beyond those services
  that typically surround the buying/selling event.
  If consumers put their trust in us to handle what
  is one of the most expensive—and most confus-
  ing—transactions of their lifetime, then what
  other services might we also perform for them?
  What else would make their lives easier—and
  help bolster our revenues?

Financing, for example, is a large part of the
real estate transaction, and financing options and
choices can be the key to the long-term success of, and
attendant customer satisfaction with, the real estate
transaction.

In the process of the real estate transaction, the
agent finds out a great deal about the client's financial position. This information could provide clues to
future business opportunities. Should this client be a
prospect for other real estate investments? Would the

purchase (or sale) of a vacation property be in order? At what point following the sale should they consider refinancing? Could refinancing be used to free up some equity for other investments? What other family members might be in need of either real estate or financial services? Are there senior citizens in the family who should perhaps be looking at some changes in their real estate holdings? Have they been introduced to the reverse mortgage—and would that fit their long-term needs?

The list goes on and on.

So how does the real estate company or individual agent make any money with all this?

It's pretty simple.

ADDING VALUE TO THE TRANSACTION

With the shift in the agent's role from the gatekeeper of information and chauffeur to the professional counselor and negotiator, we need to be learning new skills, particularly with regard to property valuation, financing, and negotiating. Those skills can serve a variety of purposes.

Should the professional real estate agent also be a financial advisor? An investment counselor? Should he/she also have a securities license and/or an insurance license? Should there be referral relationships established between the real estate practitioners and other professional service providers—relationships that will not only provide a mutually beneficial flow of clients back and forth, but that could also provide direct revenues by way of "finders fees" or some transaction-based commission structures?

There will be ongoing debate over RESPA and just how the real estate licensee might be able to receive fees for the handling or referring of business to other providers. It would be a mistake to assume that all of the restrictions currently in place will remain so indefinitely. There will be ever-increasing pressure on regulators to relax many of the restrictions currently in place, particularly as Wall Street replaces Main Street in the ownership of dominant national real estate companies and franchise organizations.

And if that is the direction of the industry, then we should be making plans right now to move in new directions to be ready to capitalize on new opportunities. If we are anticipating that payment for referred business will be legal in the future, then why not begin tightening up our referral relationships with attorneys, mortgage companies, CPAs, home inspection companies, etc? What begins as a handshake relationship with an agreement to refer clients back and forth without fees could turn into a rather lucrative network as the rules change.

And if we have missed the call here and the rules do not change, the net result will be not only increased business through client referrals, but also a higher level of service to our clients, as they will experience not only the ease and convenience of one-stop real estate shopping, but also peace of mind, knowing that a team of professionals will be at their disposal far beyond the duration of the real estate transaction itself.

Strategic planning regarding the future of the "one-stop" shopping concept needs to take into consideration the changes that have been taking place within the industry with regard to ownership of real estate companies.

One of the largest and most diversified companies ever to enter the real estate arena is Cendant, with control of the Century 21, Coldwell Banker and ERA brands. A sister company, NRT, Inc., is the nation's largest residential real estate brokerage firm, with more than seven hundred offices and annual (1998) transaction volume of more than $84 billion. Cendant Mobility (resulting from the acquisition of Homequity and subsequent merger with the relocation management companies of the individual Cendant franchises) is recognized as the largest relocation management company in the world.

Cendant itself is the result of the merger of HFS, Inc. (Hotel Franchise Systems, Inc.), owner of some of the largest names in the hotel, motel and car rental businesses, and CUC, Inc., a massive consumer marketing and database management company.

As might be expected, the company has focused on developing an affinity marketing business that would use the millions of customer contacts already in its database to attract an array of "affinity partners" who want to access to those customers. These affinity partners provide discounts and other benefits as both an added value for the consumer dealing with a Cendant-related company, and as a means of producing a significant additional revenue stream from the fees paid to Cendant by merchandisers and other service providers wanting to mine the company's rich customer base.

So, from the industry viewpoint, there is little doubt that there will be a push toward one-stop shopping and affinity marketing. But will customers want to do business with these affinity partners?

Our guess is a definite, but qualified "yes"—provided all three of the following occur:

1) the products and services are of high quality;
2) there is both real and perceived convenience in the relationship; and
3) there is some real cost saving as a result.

The latter, cost saving, is probably the least consideration, with convenience and value ranked much higher in the consumer's mind. This means that the discounting does not have to be all that great in order for the consumer to see the service as a value-added benefit in the transaction.

WHO ELSE WANTS OUR CUSTOMER?

Mass merchandisers such as Sam's Club and Costco Wholesale have also been nosing around the real estate transaction and it is likely that Wal-Mart and others may follow. In 1997, Costco, a membership buying club operating primarily on the east and west coasts, rolled out a program to provide mortgage, real estate, title and other related services to its membership at discounted rates. The program was developed in conjunction with AmeriNet, one of the earliest "lender-neutral" mortgage networks.

The real estate industry in general opposed such programs, and lobbied legislatures and real estate regulators to ban programs which charged a fee to the real estate company in order to provide a rebate for buyers or sellers. The argument: "If we have to discount our commissions, then we will not be able to provide full real estate services and the consumer will ultimately be the loser." Some brokers even argued that discounted commission schedules could force real estate companies out of business, because they were already operating on such thin margins. (I suspect the small retailers could have made the same argument as the discount malls appeared on the scene.)

In 1999, Amerinet became "HomeSpace.Inc" and launched a Web site (www. homespace.com) to provide what the company describes as "a full-service homeowner's portal" and "a consumer's one-stop e-commerce site" for real estate home loans and a variety of home services, all accessible either by Internet or a toll-free call. The site combines the attraction of discounted rates on real estate services, mortgages, moving, insurance, home warranties and inspections, with the "high touch" services of a consumer's advocate assigned to the customer throughout the homeownership cycle.

While the actual dollar savings to the end-user is undoubtedly part of the attraction of such programs, there seems to be a greater focus on marketing the advantage of a single point of contact for all the services relating to the transaction—and to other aspects of homeownership going beyond the transaction.

Take, for example, the "Home Connections" program launched in 1999 by HomeServices.Com, the nation's second-largest residential real estate brokerage firm. Home Connections is a service whereby HomeServices arranges for the connection at closing of basic home services necessary to the home buyer, such as long-distance telephone service, cellular telephone service, home security, insurance, electricity, gas, waste disposal, newspaper delivery and Internet service. Customers benefit from the service, and the company generates additional income by providing marketing and advertising services through its Home Connections e-commerce program.

If affinity marketing is attractive to the consumer, it will certainly work for the companies that are creating those programs. And if it holds out enough promise of profit for those companies, they will find a way to make it attractive to the consumer!

UNBUNDLING SERVICES

Will consumers continue to be willing to pay as much for real estate services as they have paid in the past? That is a growing concern within the real estate industry.

The question is pivotal to the future of the brokerage industry as we know it today, as a great many real estate companies are already operating on extremely thin margins and could not survive a drop in commissions.

But that is no more a concern of the consumer than was the plight of the small corner grocer when the supermarkets came to town.

The answer to both the consumer's desire to save money and the brokerage firm's need for profitability might center on the kinds of services the consumer really needs and the manner in which they are offered—and priced.

Keeping all services "bundled" in the traditional listing agreement is a "one-size-fits-all" approach to real estate services. And for many homeowners, it might still be the most attractive and effective approach.

However, consider the fact that nearly twenty-five percent of all real estate transactions are already being done without the services of a real estate brokerage firm. Could that be because a certain segment of the market rejects the "one-size-fits-all" approach? And would these same customers utilize some of the services of the real estate company if they were offered as part of a "menu" of services?

And if the existing list of services traditionally bundled together were not only unbundled, but expanded, providing even a wider variety of services (just like the mass merchandisers), would the net effect be better for both consumer and brokerage firm?

Another question revolves around who should be offering these services. Should some of the services traditionally rendered by the real estate company and agent be handed off to other parties in the transaction? Either lesser-paid employees of the real estate company or other service vendors entirely? Should some of the functions be handled by the buyers and sellers themselves?

Should the transaction be broken down into its component parts and "repackaged" for the consumer? How would this affect the cost of doing business? And would the customers go for it?

While we may have visited these questions many times in the past, given the changes that are rapidly occurring in the marketplace, our answers today may be entirely different.

In the past, prior to the information explosion of the '90s and the entry of "outsiders" into the real estate business, traditional brokers held fast to the "bundled" concept, knowing that the proprietary MLS gave them control of the information the consumer needed and that they could call their own shots as to how that information would be made available.

In today's information age, where that information has literally become the property of the end user, that proprietary "edge" has been removed. The entire concept of "unbundling" might well be a subject that needs to be revisited.

And if agents are focused on the broader range of real estate and financial services, including investment real estate opportunities, then the company should also provide a full range of property management services—or have a contractual arrangement with a property management company—one in which the management company pays a finders fee or commission on all business referred through the real estate agency. This fee would come off the top, not be added on, so that the consumer has the benefit of true one-stop shopping without paying extra for it, while the real estate company has yet another profit center to help support the one-stop configuration.

The property management company benefits from the volume of business that will be driven by the real estate company. The real estate company benefits from being able to provide these additional services.

Since the volume of first-time buyers is on the upswing, the opportunity for "fixer-upper" sales will increase.

As a percentage of first-time buyers will be going into the lower end of the resale market, purchasing homes that may not fully suit their needs for the long term but that will at least get them into homeownership, some unique opportunities for the remodeling and related service industries (painting, plumbing, room additions, kitchens, baths, etc.) will be cropping up.

The real estate company that has relationships with craftsmen and contractors in a variety of disciplines can benefit from cross-referrals with these tradesmen who often are the first to learn of a pending move when owners inquire about fixing up the properties for sale.

These relationships can also increase the salability of many of their listings in two ways:

First, having the contractors available to provide estimates for fix-ups that need to be done—either before the house is put on the market or when a buyer has been found.

Second, and perhaps even more valuable, providing drawings, floor plans, estimates, etc. for remodeling and room additions on listings that may have much greater potential.

Consider, for example, the two-bedroom, bath-and-a-half, that could quite easily be converted into a three-bedroom two-and-a-half bath home. Having the plans and estimates available to potential buyers might make the listing attractive to a wider audience. The work could be contracted for by the buyer at the time of purchase. Or, more likely, the buyer will purchase the home with the intention of doing the additions at some point in time down the road—when the space is needed and when more funds become available.

Follow-up may indicate that after living in the home for a few years, the buyer decides not to renovate, but to look for something bigger and better, creating yet another listing and sale opportunity.

Or the buyer may decide to move ahead with the renovations, perhaps creating the opportunity for refinancing to cover the costs or taking a home equity loan for the same purpose. If the company provides mortgage services, then there is another opportunity for a commissionable transaction and/or to generate revenues through cross selling of mortgage products.

From the consumer's vantage point, the ability to continually go back to the real estate agent and/or company for whatever needs or opportunities occur can be perceived as a great benefit.

All of this hinges, however, on accumulating under one umbrella a wide variety of services, all provided at competitive pricing, all performed in a timely and professional fashion, and all generating direct or indirect revenues for both the agents and the company.

A tall order? Not necessarily, but one that will take a great deal of planning.

Which services should the company provide "in house" and which should be done through referrals to other contractors?

What should the relationship with outside contractors be: subcontractors, with all work supervised by the real estate company (or another company or division owned by the real estate company); or independent contractors, each dealing with and billing the homeowner directly?

If one-stop shopping is to become a reality, a key consideration will be the importance of selecting only the very best service providers and having contractual relationships that not only provide for a revenue stream back to the real estate company, but that assure that the consumer will get the highest possible service, in the most timely fashion available, and at prices that are truly competitive. Whatever finders fees or other commissions might be passed on to the real estate company will have to be taken off the top, not added on.

In order for the program to work, the consumer must truly believe that there is a real benefit in using the real estate agent or company as the single point of contact for all services related to the process of homeownership.

And the real estate company and agent must be willing to adapt to this new mode of service delivery and reconstruct existing structures (and mindsets!) to both accommodate and profit from these emerging consumer opportunities.

REACHING THE CUSTOMER

Surveys have shown that consumers are sick and tired of mailboxes jammed with "junk" mail from everyone from the local pizzeria to attorneys, medical centers, and, yes, real estate agents.

They are even more tired of the barrage of phone calls—some with a real person at the other end, some just an automated message—interrupting their evening or weekend hours at home.

They don't want to hear about an agent's success stories. They don't want to hear that you are the biggest and best company in town. They don't care that you have been in business for half a century or that the company was founded by your great, great grandfather whose father was a decorated Civil War Veteran.

But they are interested in information that they feel may be helpful in managing their investment in real estate, helping them buy right, sell right, refinance, leverage their investment or do a multitude of other things connected with homeownership.

And they want this information when they want it, and delivered in a manner that suits their schedule.

AUTOMATED INFORMATION DELIVERY

Do consumers like automated information services?

That depends on a number of factors.

First of all, if the automated delivery system puts that information at the consumer's fingertips twenty-four hours a day, seven days a week, then the answer is most definitely yes, provided, however that other criteria are met. The information must be easily accessed—and without a lot of waiting. Busy signals and retrieval menus that are overly complex will quickly devalue the service—or at least the consumer's perception thereof.

Second, when the necessary information has been received, there needs to be a convenient procedure for moving to the next step. How do we order this service? How do we get in touch with a representative? On a telephone-based system, for example, one should be able to press one key (usually star or pound key) and be connected immediately to a service representative's pager or voice mail. And those messages should be returned within minutes, not hours, of the initial call.

If the system is Web based, filling in an e-mail address should generate an immediate e-mail reply, followed up by a phone call, fax or mailing (or some combination of all of the above) from the agent as apropos.

It has to be easy. It has to be fun. It has to be quick.

And, most of all, it has to produce the kind of access to information and/or service that the consumer is looking for.

And if tomorrow's real estate brokerage firms and agents are not able to deliver information in the manner in which the consumer wants it, you can bet that someone else will.

Chapter 3:

The Agent of the Future

The services of the professional real estate agent will still be needed, under just about any future scenario that one might envision. However, the role the real estate agent plays will most likely change— as will the number of agents filling that role.

THE NUMBER OF AGENTS WILL CHANGE

The number of real estate agents —or perhaps we should say real estate licensees—will be changing dramatically during the first decade of the twenty-first century. Over the past two decades, pundits have been predicting some shrinking within the ranks of the industry—and some noticeable shrinking has in fact occurred. Looking at the first twenty years of the new millennium, however, "shrinking" does not adequately describe what we think the future might hold. "Decimating" might be a better term!

Why this dire prediction?

Before attempting to justify my position here, let me first say that I'm not sure that it should be categorized as "dire." Rather, it should be seen as an indication that the industry is finally moving toward serious professionalism, and that the many hangers-on who have been dabbling in the business will be moving out of the ranks of the real estate agent—but not necessarily leaving the industry altogether.

What follows will hopefully put all this into better perspective:

Let's begin by taking a look at the number of transactions that will likely be available to the industry over the next ten to twenty years.

While there may be some variation in the exact number of resale unit sales forecast for the next two decades, most analysts are in agreement that the numbers will not change drastically. Some are predicting annual resales to cap at around 5.5 million by 2010; others say the numbers will rise only modestly during that period, to perhaps 5.3 million; while yet others feel that we are at a high right now and the numbers will stay relatively flat at around 5 million.

The rationale behind the forecasts involves not only general population growth, but also a number of variables, such as: the graying of America, with a much higher percentage of the overall population reaching the over-fifty-five mark; the effect on family formation as the "baby busters" and "gen-Xers" move into and out of the homebuying marketplace; and some significant increases in homeownership among the growing immigrant population.

We do not pretend to be demographers or economists, so we will leave those arguments to the experts. Suffice it to say, however, that none of the experts are predicting any significant swelling in family formation nor, therefore, any consequent increase in home sales beyond the 5.5 million mark during the next two decades.

While I tend to think that the lower numbers—around 5 million—will prove to be more accurate, for the purposes of this exercise let's accept the premise that there will be roughly 5.5 million resale transactions annually during the opening decades of the twenty-first century.

Our second premise will be based on patterns of activity of sales agents as witnessed in the closing years of the 1990s.

It has been a truism in the industry that eighty percent of the business has been done by twenty percent of the agents. During the latter half of the '90s, most industry watchers moved those numbers even further apart, saying that nearly ninety percent of the business is now being done by only ten percent of the agents.

This has been the result of a number of factors:

First, top producing agents have learned to build their own "business units" within the company, hiring personal assistants to handle a great deal of the details involved in each transaction and freeing them up to handle an increasing client load.

Second, advances in technology—voice mail and paging services, cellular and e-mail communications, Internet access to up-to-the-minute listing inventories, instant desktop publishing capabilities, etc.— have made the process of client development and holding the transaction together much more efficient.

However, all this takes an investment in equipment and in learning to use that equipment (or hiring folks who already know how)—an investment that the part-timers either cannot afford or, because of their involvement with other non-real-estate endeavors (like a full time job elsewhere), may not even consider.

Most of these changes occurred within only the last half of the closing decade of the twentieth century. (The Internet did not become a consumer commodity until 1995.) In keeping with the theory we have been advancing throughout this book, the pace of change that is the result of technological advances is just beginning to pick up and will accelerate at ever faster speeds over the next decade.

And so our next premise is that the real estate agent of the future will be able to handle an increasing number of transactions without increasing the number of hours personally dedicated to the business. (To quote an old saw, they'll be "working smarter, not harder.")

So, how many agents are active in the business today?

There are more than a million real estate licensees in the United States today. Approximately seven hundred thousand of them are members of the National Association of Realtors. Included among them are: Licensed officers and executives of companies dealing with real estate; sales managers who are not themselves actively listing and selling; property managers; and a number who are basically inactive, except perhaps for doing an occasional transaction involving a neighbor or family member.

Statistics compiled by the National Association of Realtors show that approximately seventy-five percent of all transactions are handled by members of the Association. Assuming 5 million total transactions, that puts the number of Realtor-assisted transactions at about 3.75 million annually.

So, let's assume that ten percent of the 700,000 Realtors are already handling ninety percent of the total volume available to the industry. That puts 3,375,000 transactions into the hands of about 70,000 Realtors, for an average of about forty-eight transactions annually for these top producers. (Figured as transaction sides, about one hundred sides per year.)

The remaining ten percent, or 375,000 transactions, is divided in some fashion among the remaining 630,000 Realtors.

Now, if agents are learning to handle more and more transactions—albeit by hiring a great number of assistants to do the work—and if technology is assisting the process by making the work more efficient— it is conceivable that these top producers could capture just a few more transactions each year.

Consider how little it would take to put virtually all of the business into the hands of just ten percent of today's agents. Divide the remaining ten percent of the available business (375,000 transactions) equally among the top ten percent of the agents. Each of the existing 70,000 top-ten-percenters would have to add only 5.4 transactions (roughly eleven transaction sides annually, or slightly less than one more transaction side each month) in order to capture one hundred percent of the available market.

CONVERGING TRENDS

Two converging trends are already impacting the agent's ability to deal with an increasing client base: The trend toward buyer agency (which really did not begin to take off until the mid '90s); and developments in voice-mail and e-mail technology.

During the early '90s, voice processing technology provided a new tool for the real estate industry. Hotlines (which were effectively mini telephone-based MLS systems) provided a means for real estate companies to put voice descriptions of their listings on a telephone system to give consumers twenty-four hour access to listing information. By identifying the four or five-digit code number included on yard signs and in classified ads, callers could access detailed information on any specific property. As with the MLS, the consumer could also use the system to search for available listings by entering the number of bedrooms, community, price range and other information about their needs and wants. The system would then begin describing any and all listings that fit the buyers' needs.

This was a beginning, but limited the prospective buyer to the listing inventory of the company sponsoring the Hotline.

A variation on that theme appeared on the scene during the last several years of the '90s—one that will probably have significant impact on real estate marketing, and specifically on the volume of buyer clients an individual agent can manage.

The new system employs both voice mail and e-mail technology to keep buyers posted as to listings that meet their specific needs. But, unlike the

Hotlines, these systems contain all of the listings on the MLS. The information is voiced in daily, as listings come on the market or as existing listings change (price reductions, special financing, etc.)

But, technology aside for a moment, let's look at how this concept plays out from the agent's point of view.

After interviewing the prospective buyer and determining specific needs and wants, the real estate agent has the buyer sign an exclusive right to represent (buyer's agency) agreement. An exclusive agreement is required, because the system is going to give the buyer complete access to inventory on the MLS, and the buyer's agent needs to be protected to assure that any subsequent purchase is done with that agent.

Anyone who still questions the validity of an "exclusive right to represent" agreement has lost sight of the history of the exclusive "listing" agreement. Sellers did not at some point suggest to the industry that they wanted this instrument. Rather, the popularity of the exclusive listing agreement developed largely as a result of the MLS. If listings were going to be shown by agents from other firms, then the listing agents needed to protect their claim to commission. The exclusive buyer listing is based on the very same principle, but applied on the other side of the equation.

Upon signing the buyer listing agreement, prospective buyers are given a voice mailbox phone number and personal access code. In addition, they may choose to have information sent to their e-mail address as it becomes available. They are instructed to check their voice mailbox (or e-mail) frequently for new listings and price reductions, giving buyers a real "heads up" on the market. (This is especially attractive in hot "seller's markets" where listings frequently bring offers shortly after appearing on the MLS.) In-house listings appear on the messaging system even before they get on the MLS, giving clients of the firm an even greater edge on those listings.

The key to the effectiveness of this system is the fact that it is customer-driven. Instead of requiring the agent to check the MLS daily (or more often) to find new listings that meet the buyer's needs, buyers are given the opportunity to do that for themselves. This not only frees up a great deal of the agent's time, but also gives buyers a sense of self-determination in the process. They can check for new listings over a lunch or coffee break, late at night or in the early morning hours—anytime that suits their schedule, twenty-four hours a day.

If a new listing sounds interesting, the buyer simply presses the star (or pound) key and the system instantly dials up the buyer's agent. The call goes directly to the agent's pager, identifying the buyer and the phone number at which the buyer can be reached at the moment.

Some buyers may prefer to take the information and "windshield" the property before paging their agent.

One of the early proponents of the system was Ralph Leino, broker/owner of Preferred Carlson Realtors in Kalamazoo, Michigan. Leino developed his system, which he dubbed "Direct Connect," as a means of addressing both the consumer's desire to be in control and to know that they have an "inside track" to new listings as they become available; and as a means to help agents get better control of their time and to allow them to handle literally dozens more buyers at the same time—while still providing a high level of service.

Leino also wanted a tool to help his agents get more buyers under exclusive right to represent agreements.

A number of variations on the "Direct Connect" theme are already in operation. Some do not utilize telephone delivery of the information, but require buyers to access the information via e-mail or on the company's Website.

Some systems require buyers to input their specific needs and wants on a special "shopping cart" page which is created specifically for the buyer on the company's Web site. The Web site then matches these requirements with listings added to the site and notifies the client of the new listings as they become available.

Some of the systems have inherited one of the drawbacks of the original Hotlines, as they contain only the company's own in-house listings. While some brokers consider this a plus rather than a minus, as it gives their listings exclusive exposure, the consumer of tomorrow (even today) will want —and by the terms of the buyer agent relationship, should have—access to everything that suits their needs.

A second drawback to the Web-based systems is one that will eventually disappear as consumers become more technology oriented. Almost without exception, every buyer today is accustomed to using the telephone keypad to access automated information.

Not every buyer is comfortable with or has access to the Internet. At least not yet.

But as the Internet moves from the PC to the TV set, and the keypad is replaced by the more familiar TV remote control, the e-commerce revolution will be in the hands of the masses, and the "Internet Empowered Consumer" will be the norm.

This is an example of one of the strategic planning principles that we are trying to drive home throughout this book—and certainly in our concluding chapter: Any new system, any new marketing technique, any new business strategies that we consider implementing should be able to pass two simple tests:

1) Does it fit the marketplace as it exists at this very moment? (Will the consumers and the agents buy into it?)

2) Will it comfortably segue into new iterations as both advancing technology and increased consumer awareness permit?

Jumping too fast into programs that the marketplace is not ready to embrace can be just as fatal as stagnating and failing to move forward with new approaches and new technology. In fact, it could be worse, as the cost of change—both in hard costs and in training and marketing costs—can double the negative effect if the marketplace is not ready to respond to the changes we've made. And, add to this, the cost of lost business as we find ourselves moving away from the marketplace rather than leading it toward us!

SO, WHAT'S LEFT FOR THE REST?

If it is true that more and more business will be concentrated in the hands of the very top echelon of sales agents, what will be left for all the rest?

We will admit that despite all the changes that may take place over the next two decades, there will always be some loners, mom-and-pops and other small niche-marketers who remain in business and carve out their share of the market. But their numbers will also shrink tremendously, both because of the cost of doing business and the expectations and perceptions of the general homebuying and selling public who will be pulled more and more by high-tech, high-touch, one-stop-shopping types of marketing.

But a great many of that category of agents whom we have dubbed "part-timers" or "marginal producers" will move into other roles within the industry. We already see them working as licensed personal assistants. Technology will produce jobs for a great number of such agents in non-sales capacities within the megabrokerage firms and even in the smaller companies, servicing the growing volume of business generated by the top producing sales agents.

So they will not altogether disappear from the industry, but will find themselves doing other jobs for which they are, in fact, much more suited, and which will, over the long haul, produce much greater career satisfaction and steady reliable income. The end result will be both increased profitability for both company and agent, as well as a much higher level of consumer service.

GEARING UP FOR THE FUTURE

For the real estate agent of today, all this should present some food for serious thought about career planning. Those who are good at sales need to either begin creating their own business plan to include personal assistants and partners to begin pushing more volume through the books, or find the organizations within which such systems are already in place and within which they can become much more productive at what they do best: getting eyeball to eyeball with clients and customers to create real estate transactions.

Those who seem less inclined to shine in the salesperson's role should begin watching for areas of specialization in which they can channel their talents and become experts—specialists who will work behind the scenes supporting the sales and marketing activities of the firm or of teams of agents within the firm.

Broker/owners and managers should look to creating the atmosphere in which such teams can develop and which will attract the top producers as a place where they can truly excel in sales. Tomorrow's real estate professionals will want to know that the infrastructure is in place not only to service the clientele which they themselves attract to the firm, but also to attract additional buyers and sellers because of the firm's ability to provide all the services that the consumer will be looking for, in the most attractive, cost-effective and consumer-friendly fashion.

The impact of all this on a recruiting program could be monumental!

If the role of the real estate professional is evolving, and good sales agents will control an ever increasing percentage of the total available volume, then it is imperative that we recruit agents who are not only good at the basic human communication skills involved in selling, but who can also adapt their techniques, work habits and business style to fit well in the evolving marketplace of tomorrow.

There may be some dyed-in-the wool top producers out there right now who are still doing very well handling all the details of the transaction themselves. They are probably working sixty or seventy hours over a seven-day work week, and running on an early burnout track doing so. There are others who have the basic selling skills but who are also amenable to—and good at—delegating, and who will zero in on the client contact details and relish the fact that more and more of the other work is being done by support staff. They will work well in a team environment and will spend more of their time in immediate income-producing activities. They will drive increasingly more business into the firm, knowing that it will all be handled very expeditiously and professionally by the entire team available in the company.

For those planning to launch into a more proprietary mode, putting together coalitions of brokers who will develop new companies along the lines of the models currently in place within the legal and medical professions, the need to work well in a team environment is equally important—as is aligning oneself with like-minded brokers who will form the nucleus of such a venture.

EVOLUTION OF CONSULTATIVE SERVICES

Whether real estate companies continue to be locally owned and operated; whether they are configured as small offices networked together or mammoth mega-offices; whether the home buyer comes into the system through agent contact or through the Internet; and regardless of how the advertising, promotion, and showing of properties is handled—it will continue to come down at some point to bringing the buyer and seller together in a "meeting of the minds" before the transaction can take place.

For this reason, we feel strongly that the role of the negotiator will become a mainstay of the real estate professional's skills. And from this role, a number of other consultative services will evolve.

If the client—buyer or seller—has placed his/her confidence in the real estate agent to structure and negotiate what is probably one of the largest financial transactions that the client will personally be involved in, then it is not much of a stretch of the imagination to think that the client will place similar confidence in that agent for other financially related decisions.

Perhaps the name that we give ourselves is a bit misleading and tends to restrict our thinking as to what our role should be. We think of ourselves as "real estate" professionals, yet we generally do not know a whole lot about the construction of homes—that is why our clients hire inspectors and engineers to assess the structural conditions of their prospective purchases.

As agents, we are not directly involved in the title search. We leave that to other experts.

We are not directly involved in the financing process. We leave that to the mortgage lenders.

We will no longer be needed to find out what is on the market—or to get information on comparable listings or even recent home sales. That is all moving into the domain of the everyday consumer, thanks to the Internet.

Not to say that we should not learn more about all these things.

Like it or not, a better description of the historical role of the real estate agent is probably "sales person." There are unique "people skills" that the sales profession requires and that successful real estate agents seem to possess.

And the fact that we are third parties to the transaction also goes a long way toward building our credibility and establishing a place for our services in the transaction.

We are not involved in the construction of the home. We are not part of the chain of title. We do not have the emotional attachment of the seller, nor are we mesmerized by the attraction that the home has for the buyer.

As such, we can act as disinterested third parties, all the while representing the best interests of the parties to the transaction.

The role of the agent as the single person taking responsibility for the success of the transaction will become even more important in the coming years, particularly as the sources of both information and services proliferate as a result of the Internet explosion.

But nothing is more critical to the outcome of the transaction, and nothing so clearly defines the role of the real estate professional, as the process of drawing the parties together in the transaction. Bringing buyer and seller into agreement over pricing, terms and timing, and doing so in a manner that all parties feel they have gotten a fair shake.

While much emphasis was placed on "agency" during the '90s, the focus in the twenty-first century is likely to shift more towards "customer representation," as the industry rallies around the "total customer experience." Developing "customers for life" will be increasingly important, particularly as major national real estate entities consolidate a variety of homeowner services under the umbrella of the real estate company.

"AGENCY" YIELDS TO "CUSTOMER REPRESENTATION"

Buyer and seller agency as we know it will not disappear. In fact, agency representation will take on even greater significance as a "value added" that the real estate professional brings to the transaction. But as we focus more on the "customer for life" scenario, the consumer will at various times be in a different relationship to the real estate transaction: sometimes the seller, sometimes the buyer, sometimes the investor, or the borrower—or even the lender. The long-term relationship of "customer" will transcend the specific customer need of the moment (buying or selling), provided the "total customer experience" has been a good one, and the real estate agent and/or company maintains an ongoing dialogue with that consumer.

The viewpoint that the real estate transaction

necessarily involves an "adversarial" relationship between buyer and seller will also change. This will be due partly to the availability of information via the Internet. Whether in the role of buyer or seller, the consumer will have a "third-party" reference of comparable pricing on a variety of Internet sites.

In the past, relying on the rather limited information on the MLS, it was difficult to know just how "comparable" listings actually were. The figures were there—acreage, overall square footage, size of rooms (though usually with the disclaimer that these might not always be reliable!), and a "windshield" picture of the home was probably included.

Today, while facts and figures on the Internet may be equally unreliable (the human error factor has not changed), multiple views of the property's exterior and interior, often 360-degree shots showing the rooms in full perspective, give visitors to these sites a much better feel for the comparability of properties.

Add to this the fact that both buyer and seller have their specific objectives, but that unless there is a win-win plan for reaching those objectives, the transaction likely will never occur.

MEDIATING A "WIN-WIN" OUTCOME

The buying and selling process more closely resembles "mediation" than "litigation." In litigation, there is generally one winner and one loser. (Actually, there are three winners and one loser if you count the law firms in the equation.) In mediation, there are two winners, as the parties have been brought to the mediation process in hopes of resolving a dispute or difficulty and leaving the table with a resolution in hand.   If an agreeable solution is not reached, the mediation process is terminated and both parties start back at square one.

The real estate transaction is quite similar. The buyer wants the house, knows the asking price and wants to make an offer. Both parties have some idea of what the resolution should be. And since both have an interest in seeing the transaction take place, they meet at the bargaining table (albeit usually through their professional representatives) to hammer out a resolution that will best meet their goals. Sometimes price is the hanger. Sometimes it is terms that cause the problem. Most often, however, both leave the table feeling that they have done as well as could be expected, given current market conditions. If a reasonable compromise cannot be reached, they walk away. Many a purchase offer has been rejected.

The process of professional representation—and the success of the "customer for life" and "total customer experience" requires that both parties feel that they have been well advised and well represented in the bargaining process. Overall market conditions, (e.g. strong "buyer's market" or "seller's market") or specific needs of one party or the other (e.g. seller or buyer has an immovable deadline, as often found in the case of relocation, divorce, or necessity to close on other transaction, etc.), could be the reason why one party or the other is disappointed with the results but moves forward anyway. But these are situations beyond the control of the real estate agents representing the parties. How well the agents are able to make the best of such situations, however, could affect the "total customer experience."

Everyone would like to walk away from a medical examination with a "clean bill of health." When there are problems, however, how well the physician explains them to the patient and the resulting course of treatment prescribed has a lot to do with the "total patient experience." The doctor is only the "messenger." But there are messengers—and then there are messengers!

The people skills extend beyond the negotiating process. The successful agent has to know how to get the potential buyer to recognize the true value of the home in question. And this relates not only to a physical appraisal of the property—a totally objective evaluation of the bricks and sticks on the lot—but also to the more subjective aspects: why this will be a good home for this specific buyer.

He/she knows how to recognize and overcome symptoms of "buyer's remorse"—keeping the deal (and the buyer) in one piece.

Always the good salesperson, the successful agent knows how to take the prospect from the role of "just looking" into that of a serious buyer; to help them move from relative passivity into an aggressive buying mode.

PROFESSIONAL/TECHNICAL KNOWLEDGE

All of these are people skills; all sales-related skills.

Then there is the role of professional knowledge: property valuation (important to both seller and buyer); knowledge of how to make financing work; how to get the best deal over both long and short haul; how to make the transaction possible even when the credit is a bit shaky or the funds a bit thin.

The agent's professional knowledge of financing will become even more important given the fact that most sales projections indicate that the first-time-buyer marketplace will become an ever more important segment of the entire real estate marketplace.

The agent of the future will need to understand much more about property management—both for those needing to rent for a while before they can buy and for the investors with property to manage. The professional agent needs to be able to identify the would-be investor and know how to help them create wealth through real estate. This is extremely important, considering the increasing number of first-time buyers, the expanding immigrant marketplace and the needs of the growing senior population.

At the same time, some of the more traditional functions by which we have defined real estate success may be disappearing.

As the property "listing" function slips from the proprietary confines of the MLS to the free public access of the Internet, the old adage "he who lists will last" will not necessarily have much validity. In the past many have become top producers by wooing a great many listing clients, knowing that if they got the listing priced right and got it into the MLS, someone would sell it. The consumer public likely will no longer be willing to pay big commissions just to get the exposure of the MLS. The focus will shift to seller "representation." "Listing" may become a simple advertising function on the Internet rather than a contractual agency-creating function.

Prospecting may also be a disappearing role—at least for the top-producing agent. While prospecting in the traditional patterns may still be a viable way to develop business, it may no longer prove to be cost-effective in light of technological advances designed to supplant it. The most successful neighborhood "farming" techniques of the past may soon be supplanted by professional marketing departments utilizing lead-generation and customer-development and maintenance techniques and technology developed for other industries.

There will be many roles that make up the real estate service delivery system—and that of the sales agent will be just one of them.

Let's face it, a skilled machinist may still be able to build an automobile, but he cannot do it as well as nor as economically as the assembly line.

It is unlikely that a medical doctor today would possess all the knowledge and skills of the medical profession. In most medical practices today medical services are delivered by a network of service providers—nurse practitioners, internists, specialists, and a large cadre of laboratory technicians and assistants focusing an enormous amount of talent and technology on the specific needs of each patient.

Those who have spent their careers honing prospecting skills and developing personal marketing systems for generating repeat and referral business may watch that business going to the mass real estate merchandisers, either because of sheer convenience of one-stop shopping or to take advantage of special discounts and deals offered by these marketing moguls.

Remember the plight of the corner grocer—the guy who carried his customers on interest-free credit on a week-to-week basis? I remember the little note pad with the carbon-copied yellow receipts that our grocer used to tally up our account when I was a boy. We'd sometimes pay cash, we'd sometimes put it all "on the cuff." And as the money became available, we'd pay our account down, and sometimes even clean it up entirely. And I am not speaking of the Depression days of the '30s, but of the booming postwar days of the '40s.

Despite the corner grocers' loyalty to their customers, when the supermarkets came to town, the little guys on the corner could watch their former customers go by on their way to bigger selections and bigger bargains. Our parents may not have been so anxious to abandon the corner grocer, but economic and social pressures gradually swayed them, as mass merchandisers established both product lines and prices that the little guy couldn't compete with. And we, the next generation, had little interest in going into the corner store, which we perceived as "dying," but headed straight for the big guys. It was a matter of selection, of time, of "one-stop" shopping (hey, these guys had hardware and prescriptions and groceries all under the same roof. They had plenty of parking, too, and a dozen or more checkout lanes.

Convenience, pricing, selection won the day. Old allegiances were quickly forgotten. A new way of doing business captured the American consumer.

So also the butcher, the baker and the candlestick maker. We now purchase all those products from the mass merchandiser.

There are still specialty stores, many of them doing quite well. Some because they carry products that aren't available at the malls—and brands and styles that cannot be comparison shopped at the mass merchandisers.

Some are still around and loyally patronized because they bring a certain element of service to the transaction—something that may seem to be missing at the discount outlets.

But their numbers are very small—and probably getting smaller with each advancing generation.

So why should the real estate agent's plight be any different? Why should he or she expect that past service will be any guarantee of future loyalty? "What else can you do for me?" will still be the governing rule. And the agent of the future will either learn to do more things or to do certain specific things in a very efficient manner, leaving much of the work previously associated with his or her role for others more suited to the task.

It will be up to the agent—and the real estate brokerage industry—to reinvent the role of the agent in the light of both what the consumer really wants and what others may be offering as competition.

For those who fine-tune their skills in the truly professional aspects of the business—such as property valuation, negotiation, financial consultation—business opportunities will be plentiful. And for a number of reasons:

First, these are skills that have not been developed by a great percentage of today's real estate salespeople. As a result, a great number of today's competitors will disappear from the scene as such skills become the predominant factor in agent selection.

Second, no matter how the real estate brokerage business is constructed, these skills will be required and will be hired in just about every imaginable scenario. And because such skills will be at a premium, those who are able to provide such services will be well compensated.

Third, because so much else of what has typically been the agent's work will be done by others—or not required at all, due to technological advances and cultural changes—the professional agent will be able to handle a much larger case load of clients at any given time, resulting in higher per-hour returns on time invested.

SERVICE BEYOND THE SALE

Beyond the income potential traditionally associated with listing and selling property, the real estate agent of the future will find opportunities in counseling the homeowner throughout his or her course of home ownership.

Beginning with the initial purchase, the real estate professional will serve in the role of counselor, advising the buyer with regard to the terms and conditions of the purchase offer, then negotiating the contract on behalf of the buyer client.

Financing will remain an essential part of most transactions, and the sales agent of the future will take a proactive role in reviewing financing options and advising clients on the mortgage instruments that best fit their long and short-term goals. While an increasing amount of mortgage information will be available via the Internet, including Web sites on which the entire mortgage transaction can be completed, the average consumer will need advice and counsel in sifting through the myriad of options.

And the role of mortgage counselor will continue after the sale. As new mortgage instruments are created, and rates change, there will be windows of opportunity in which the homeowner can improve his or her position by refinancing. Further, the equity built up in the home could also be leveraged into other investments, including a second home, vacation or retirement property—all of which become both investment opportunities for the homeowner and commissionable opportunities for the agent who sees the buyer as a "customer for life." (See Chapter Five.)

Or consider the rapidly growing senior citizen marketplace. Should we be knowledgeable enough to counsel our clients in this age category on such things as the pros and cons of reverse mortgages, or ways to structure real estate holdings to assure the highest returns—both for income while living and for estate planning purposes?

"But that is the role of the financial planners," you say. Perhaps so—today. But is that by default, because we as professionals have chosen not to enter that arena? Should some agents move into these areas of specialization? Or should the real estate professional refer the client to others within the "full service" firm who specialize in these areas?

If we truly want to be considered experts in our field, then there are many opportunities to be of service and to generate commissions—provided, of course that:

- We have the knowledge and professional expertise.
- Our clients recognize that expertise.
- We have working relationships with a variety of related service providers.

Should the real estate company and agent be in the mortgage business? Of course, if it will benefit our client base!

Should the real estate company and agent be the link to many other services—everything from insurance, to home security services, to lawn and pool care services?

Of course, as long as our clients will benefit from our ability to provide such a "one-stop" service.

Does the typical buyer or seller want to shop on her own for all the related services? Probably not. But should they be free to do so? Of course. But if we are going to hold ourselves out as the "one source" for a variety of homeowner's needs, then we had better know those businesses well, and establish strong relationships with a variety of service providers who are very good at what they do.

Should we be able to get paid for our involvement with that broader base of homeowner related services? Of course we should, just as any other service provider. And even more so, since we also provide not only the convenience of a "one source" supplier, but also the ability to sort through all the various options and recommend those that will be of most value to our clients.

The *concierge* services that are being developed by some real estate companies today are based on the concept that buyers and sellers are busy with many things—their lives are not centered around the real estate transaction—and that it will be beneficial to our clients to have all such services available through a single source.

There are other benefits, however, that may not be as obvious, such as the benefit of quality control. Whereas the supplier of a service (e.g. home inspection) may see the individual homeowner as just one of a great many individual customers, the real estate company and/or agent will be seen by the supplier as a source of a volume of business—an ongoing stream of business. This should impact not only the pricing of the service but also the timeliness and quality of the service delivery. If a home inspector or appraiser drops the ball with an individual customer, he runs the risk of losing that one customer—a customer whom he will probably not see again, anyway. Drop the ball with a client of the real estate company, however, and you run the risk of losing the volume of business that company can bring you. There's a big difference. And it can translate into a tremendous consumer benefit.

Any decisions on ancillary businesses or affinity relationships should be based not on the question, "What else can I sell?" but rather on the question, "What else does my client need?" Over the years, real estate sales people have often worried that it would be demeaning to sell other services. They saw themselves as real estate professionals and felt their focus should be restricted to services traditionally associated with buying or selling a home. "We should just keep doing what we have always been known to do," they would reason.

The viewpoint of tomorrow is shifting toward a

consumer-centric one in which the client's overall needs are taken into consideration —a "holistic" approach to the client as both homeowner and investor in real estate.

The consumer may buy a house as shelter, but it is also an investment. It is both an asset, and a liability. The consumer is at once the buyer (selecting the home); the financier (investing the down payment); the mortgagor (guaranteeing the payments); the property manager (keeping the shrubs trimmed, getting the roof fixed); the accountant (paying the bills, keeping tax records); and the CFO (Is this asset appreciating? How should it be leveraged? Are our liabilities covered?).

For most homeowners, these roles are played only by default. The home is neither their business nor their hobby. They got into this "business" only because they needed a place to live!

Viewed strictly from the viewpoint of the home buyer and seller, the "one-stop" concept begins to come into clearer perspective.

This is not to say that the real estate professionals of tomorrow will have their hands in all of those businesses. But it does say that they will have to have a clear understanding of all the businesses related to homeownership (including the ability to analyze the financial aspects of the sale), and have connections with the suppliers of all those related services.

And the company or agent who is able to provide a true "one source" service will be perceived as adding a great deal of value to the transaction—a value that will command a commensurate price.

We can sit back and say that none of this is really going to happen, and then watch others from outside our industry take the ball and run with it.   In that scenario, the best we can hope for is the crumbs that fall from their tables. (Remember how third-party relocation and advance marketing companies ate our lunch!) Or, we can take a proactive stance that will enhance and protect our position and pre-empt outsiders from wresting away our control.

WILL THE INTERNET INTERVENE?

As we go into the new millennium, the real estate industry is still very much in control of the customer. The customer may be browsing the Internet, but still comes to the Realtor to make the transaction happen.

Remember that the typical buyer and seller is not in the real estate business and does not consider real estate his or her hobby. That is why having direct access to listings on the Internet (instead of needing to go through a Realtor to get to the MLS) has not greatly impacted the FSBO marketplace. There are still about the same number of sellers who are taking this route. Some are utilizing a variety of Web sites to achieve their purposes. But we have not yet seen a dramatic conversion to the FSBO mentality.

However, there are also a great many related service providers who are eyeing the buyer/seller consumer and devising ways to wrest control of the "gateway" to this customer away from the Realtor.

Unfortunately, the real estate industry as a whole took a "protectionist" approach, first trying to prevent direct consumer access, then, when prevention proved impossible, trying to control that access on proprietary systems.

As Internet services expanded in the late '90s, and as consumers became more involved with the World Wide Web, the real estate industry made a number of missteps. First, there was a movement to maintain strict control of the MLS at all costs! "We cannot allow this proprietary information to get into the hands of others as this has been our means of maintaining control of the customer—and the marketplace."

But information has a way of getting out and, despite our best efforts, it soon became obvious that the old world was disappearing. The next movement was to accept the fact that the MLS had to migrate to the Internet and become a global database rather than thousands of unrelated local sites.

The industry's knee-jerk reaction then was to find a way to create a proprietary Web site that would make the information available to consumers, but keep it out of the hands of the enemy—whoever or whatever that might prove to be. (I tend to agree with Walt Kelley's conclusion, as expressed through his cartoon character Pogo: "We has met the enemy—and they is us!") There followed a great many attempts to restrict listings to a specific site and to prevent practitioners from utilizing the ever broadening array of sites on which their seller's property could be exposed.

At this writing, the mood seems to be shifting, and common sense is beginning to prevail. Let's look at this thing from the consumer's viewpoint rather than our own. If the number of Web sites on which homes for sale might be found are proliferating, and if consumers will be attracted to those sites for whatever reasons, then it only makes sense to see that our sellers' properties are listed on all of them—provided, of course, the cost does not outweigh the benefit. (An easy call, as long as the listings remain free!)

In the beginning of the Internet wars over control of real estate listings, there was fear that "outsiders" such as Microsoft were going to "eat our babies." If we consider the "babies" to be real estate listing information, those "babies" are already gone! In the Internet Age, information is truly owned by its user, not its creator.

The question we should be attempting to answer—as an industry and as individual real estate agents—is how can we position ourselves as professionals to maintain control of the customer—not the information—within this rapidly changing milieu? And the answer to that question will only be found by putting the customer first. The customer will be "owned" by whatever entities prove to provide the best overall customer experience, including product knowledge, service, availability and, above all, accountability.

What does the customer need?

What does the customer want?

What will be good for the customer?

Equally important is a keen understanding of just where the customer may be at any given point along the way. What is the customer's current perception of what is good for him? What factors are influencing that perception? How can we—or should we—become involved in forming that perception?

Let's look at another example. During the latter half of the decade of the '90s, affinity marketing programs came into prominence, including those developed by the relocation management industry or created by major national real estate franchising entities, and others that cropped up from the mortgage side of the business. While these programs each had its own specific twist, the common denominator of them all was to capture the consumer marketplace by providing some form of discount, rebate or other benefit that would be perceived to be of value by the consumer.

Another common denominator was that these programs, by and large, were to be financed at least in part by referral fees paid by the real estate brokers.

The knee-jerk reaction of the real estate industry was to oppose these programs—not because the rebates and discounts themselves were bad for the consumer, but because they posed an economic threat to the industry. "The bottom line profitability of most brokerage firms is already quite tenuous," the reasoning went. "We will not be able to continue to operate—or at least to continue to provide a high level of service—if our commissions are seriously discounted."

Think back to the relocation scenario described in Chapter One. Our thinking as an industry was way off track when we focused on getting third-party listings as the primary objective, totally missing the fact that what the customer (i.e. the corporate employer) really needed—and would pay handsomely for—was a way to keep those third-party listings from ever materializing!

As the mom and pop retailers of the past discovered, consumers will not only get what they want, but may want something totally different from what we have been giving them. If some entity comes on the scene that can provide what the consumer wants (or can make the consumer want what they provide), the traditional vendors will find their business disappearing down the street to that new entity.

If there is such pressure on commissions that our brokerage operations will not be able to deliver the level of service to which our customers have become accustomed, then there are several possible solutions (short of just going out of business) that I can think of:

1) Find a way to continue to provide all those services, but more efficiently and at a lower cost.

2) Re-define the specific services that the real estate agent is uniquely positioned to offer, and develop our business around just those services.

3) Find others who can benefit from our connecting them with the customer and who will be willing to participate in the costs.

4) A combination of all of the above.

In any event, we need to understand that while the real estate agent will no longer be the gatekeeper, what the Internet provides is just data, information. What the consumer really needs is knowledge and understanding that comes from being able to sift through all that data and interpret it. The real estate agent should be the conduit for that.

THE BUCK STOPS HERE

Also important, and something that is given too little attention, is the role of the agent as the one person who uniquely takes responsibility for the entire transaction—before, during and beyond settlement.

We can get all kinds of medical information from the Internet, but we still want a medical doctor who is a specialist in his field to diagnose our problems and supervise their treatment. We want the professional to have all the knowledge that is on the Internet. And we may be asking many more informed questions about our illness and its remedies as a result of our access to information on the Internet. But we still rely on our doctor as the professional.

If the role of the real estate professional is to survive in the new information age, it will only do so for those agents who are prepared to become truly professional counselors; who know where to get information and how to interpret it; who can either accomplish everything related to the transaction or know how and to whom to refer; and who are willing and able to assume responsibility for the overall well being of the consumer as buyer, seller and homeowner.

Anything less than that becomes merely a commodity—and one that will have little value in the new scheme of things.

Chapter 4:

The Company of the Future

Now that we have examined the changes taking place in the consumer marketplace and the consequent evolving role of the real estate agent, it is time to take a look at the real estate brokerage management business itself: What will the real estate company of the future look like?

Let's start by saying what it will NOT look like—and that is very simple: It will not resemble the structure to which we have all become so accustomed over the years:

- The relationship with the consumer will be changed;
- The relationship between agent and brokerage firm will be changed;
- And the relationships among agents themselves will evolve as well.

It is also safe to say that, just as in the past, there will not be one single format within which all brokerage operations will operate.

We have always had a wide variety of forms, including the very small mom-and-pop company, with perhaps only a husband-and-wife broker team or just one or two agents. At the other end of the spectrum have come the massive "megabrokerage" firms, with dozens of offices and a multitude of agents.

Neither of these will altogether disappear from the scene, but both will change radically in the way they are put together and function.

The total number of real estate companies (and offices) will likely be reduced, as mergers and acquisitions continue to consolidate the industry.

WHO WILL OWN THE CUSTOMER?

Any attempt to foresee what the real estate company of tomorrow will look like must deal with the pivotal question of who will control the customer.

Today, there is little doubt that the individual agents have control. The signs are all around in the advertising and marketing that reaches the consumer.

Yard signs were once emblazoned with the company name and phone number, and *sometimes* carried a rider with the listing agent's name. Today, yard signs feature the individual agent, sometimes even with a full-color photograph. The agent's personal phone number, pager number and e-mail address are there for the consumer to copy. The company name is also there, but often in much smaller type and with much less prominence.

Most of the direct mail that reaches the consumer's mailbox is also "personal marketing" developed by the individual agent: brochures, flyers, newsletters—all promoting the agent. At the open house, property brochures and other information all carries the personalization of the agent.

The current control of the customer by the agent has come about more by default than by plan. It is more the result of *evolutionary* progress than of *revolutionary* action. However, going into the twenty-first century, many converging trends could make this issue the focus of strategic planning and create entirely new relationships between the consumer, the companies providing real estate services and the licensees delivering those services.

Among them:

- Increasing independence of the individual licensed agent;
- Disappearing bottom-line profitability of the typical brokerage firm engaged in "traditional" real estate practices;
- Advances in communications technology, particularly central server data storage and delivery systems;
- Entrance of many outside players into the residential real estate arena, bringing concepts such as "branding," "total customer experience" and "shareholder value" into the mix.

It is our prediction that the question of control of the customer will likely be one of the major issues that will shape the future of the real estate industry over the next decade.

CAPTURING MARKET SHARE

The question of control of the customer goes beyond just the issue of how agents are identified. It speaks to the larger question of whether or not the company is achieving its full potential in capturing market share. If prospecting for new business is left solely to the marketing efforts of the individual agents, the company may be leaving a lot of business on the table. Similarly, if following up with leads is left strictly to the agents, a great deal of potential profit may be slipping through the cracks. And all this represents lost business, not only for the company, but for the individual agents as well.

As managers, can we account for all of the consumers who call the company seeking information or assistance? Not just the ones coming into the company's own switchboard, but all of the calls and messages to individual agents' pagers, home phones, voice mails or e-mails?

We may know how many sellers are under contract with the company at any given time. Our listing files should provide that information. But do we know how those sellers are being serviced? How well are the properties being marketed? What kind of communication is going on between the company and those clients? Do we have any idea how many buyers the company is working with at any given time, and how those buyers are being handled?

Is there any way of knowing how many former customers are being lost to our competition through inefficient or nonexistent client follow-up procedures?

If we are going to relegate control of the customer to the individual agent, then systems need to be in place to be sure those customers are not being lost. Developing and implementing those systems should be an integral part of the service the real estate company supplies to its agents.

A further problem of total agent control of the customer is the agent's ability to take that customer along when moving to another firm. The portability of the agent's license creates portability of the company's customer base as well. Not to mention the "bargaining power" that it puts on the agent's side when negotiating commission splits.

Many broker-owners have already decided that there is no way to change this situation. The customers have come to know the individual agents, they reason, and customer loyalty will therefore go with the agent, not the company. Attempting to change that structure could alienate agents and precipitate a mass exodus of both agents and their customers.

This could happen, and is a serious consideration for anyone who decides to gain back control. But how that control is gained back, and what the net effect is to the agents will be the determining factor.

One option would be to continue to see the agent as the customer of the company, and to use the company's lead development programs to feed more real estate business to its agents.

Economy of scale should give the real estate firm an edge over the individual real estate agent in harnessing Internet and central server technology to create consumer marketing and lead development programs. Developing advanced marketing techniques, using not only the latest in technology but also a professional marketing staff, could give the company a decided edge in generating qualified buyer and seller leads. This would not only put the company back in control of the consumer, but could also put the company in a much stronger position with regard to agent recruiting and retention, as these qualified leads could be provided to individual agents to augment the business they are already developing on their own.

In this configuration, the company may opt to continue existing commission splits, profiting only indirectly from the agent loyalty that a lead-generation system will develop. Direct profits would then flow from the non-real estate business opportunities created with this expanded customer base.

Or, the company could decide to generate additional profit from this new source of customers by charging its agents referral fees for any leads thus developed. (This would be patterned after "affinity" marketing programs already in place within the national franchise organizations.)

The same effect could be accomplished by establishing a dual commission structure: a higher split for leads developed directly by the agent; lower for those developed by the company and assigned to the agent.

Some companies may opt to have a separate staff to handle all of the leads generated by the marketing department. Agents to whom these leads are assigned might be new recruits who have not yet developed their own personal marketing network. Or, they could be more seasoned agents who are more interested in working directly with qualified customers than in spending their time prospecting.

The key to success will lie in demonstrating that the company is better equipped to employ certain techniques for capturing the consumer's attention than is the individual agent. New marketing programs developed by the company should be viewed by the agents as a means to augment existing business, not as a replacement for the business they develop on their own.

A "partnering" approach will no doubt work best in this regard. The company's decision not to leave any potential business on the table should be "sold" to the agents in such a way that it is not perceived as putting the company in competition with its agents, but rather in partnership with them to create a much larger volume of business—and higher bottom-line incomes for both company and individual agent.

A more drastic approach would be to see the consumer as the customer of the company, and the sales agents as a means of providing specific services on a fee basis. In this configuration, leads would be parceled out to licensed agents whose function would be to provide whatever personal services necessary to complete the transaction (client counseling, structuring and negotiation of offers, etc.), while salaried personnel would handle all of the administrative details.

The licensees utilized in the process could be employees of the firm or totally independent contractors who are under contract to handle this business. (Not unlike the relationships that major merchandisers such as Sears or Home Depot have established with independent home improvement contractors.)

This configuration would likely be adopted by companies that have not been in the residential real estate business, but see this as an add-on to their existing businesses. Wal-Mart, for example, where millions of consumers are already coming through the doors weekly, might see some opportunity to reap additional profits from providing real estate services to its existing customer base.

TRACKING THE CUSTOMER

There is another element that needs to be built into any company-directed marketing and lead development programs: ongoing control through the development of rather sophisticated customer tracking programs. While leads may be parceled out to individual agents in a variety of fashions, all such leads need to be tracked—not only to the conclusion of the transaction, but beyond. The customer needs to be seen as the customer of the company for life.

This becomes even more important as real estate companies find themselves moving into the full-service, "one-stop-shopping" arena, with a variety of potential profit centers beyond the traditional commission for representing the buyer or seller. While the individual agents may focus solely on the real estate transaction, the company needs to be focused on the broader aspects of the consumer as homeowner and customer for an array of products and services, ranging from home products and services (warranties, security systems, lawn and pool care services, etc.) to a full range of financial services (insurance, mortgage financing, refinancing, home equity loans, etc.)

The more diversified the product and service base of the real estate company becomes, the more essential the need for taking control of the customer base.

HOW MANY & HOW BIG?

There are quite divergent opinions about what will happen to the size of each individual office. Advances in communications technology would dictate that space traditionally allocated for individual agents' activities—desks, cubicles, semiprivate or private offices—will all but disappear from the floor plan, as more work is done in cyberspace and less in office space.

This would seem to dictate that office size will shrink. But not necessarily so.

If the real estate company moves into a "one-stop shopping" mode, a number of related businesses or service groups may be housed in the same office—either company-owned business units or "strategic partners" who lease office space (and other services) from the real estate company.

As the real estate transaction becomes "unbundled," a variety of "specialists" will be performing the various tasks associated with the transaction. Most of these will operate from within the office. Even many of the tasks now performed in the clients' homes or at the property listings—especially initial counseling of either buyer or seller—will be performed in client counseling rooms within the real estate office.

The total personnel count in each office will likely expand, but that does not mean there will be more "real estate agents." In today's office, support staff grows as agent count grows, as many agents are hiring their own personal assistants, many of whom are working in the real estate office.

In the office of the future, the agent population—those licensed professionals who are doing the specific functions of client counseling and negotiating the transaction ("bringing buyers and sellers together")—will probably decline. Each agent will be doing a smaller portion of the total work traditionally associated with the transaction, but handling a great many more transactions.

However, the number of support personnel will grow, as much of the work previously handled by licensed sales agents will now come under the job description of a variety of specializations.

The size of the office and the functions it serves will also depend largely upon the company's decision regarding ownership of the customer. If, as we suspect, the trend is toward moving control of the customer away from the individual agent and back to the company (albeit in some form of "partnership" with the agents), then a variety of other services will become native to the real estate office—although not necessarily to each branch office. In larger companies, these likely will be centralized functions, particularly given the advances in communications, Internet and Intranet services.

MULTI-OFFICE EXPANSION

While megabrokers will continue to grow through merger and acquisition, some smaller companies may take the traditional path of expansion through opening new offices. In some cases, this expansion will involve bringing existing personnel into an ownership position in order to generate the capital necessary to branch out.

In some cases, "teams" will be created within

the main office, then transplanted to the new location. Team leaders may be given some ownership in the new entity and an opportunity to purchase even more.

An "angel investor" concept may come into play, whereby the hub retains one hundred percent ownership in the branch as long as the seed capital needed to start the branch is still at risk. Once that capital has been returned, a percentage of ownership is transferred to the branch "owners" (team leaders, others who qualify to own stock in the company) based on bottom line performance benchmarks. In the end, the hub will retain a minority position in the branch, with agreements specifying how profits will be distributed.

The hub would expand to provide services for each of the spokes or branches, creating economy of scale in many operations that can be done more efficiently and economically centrally rather than locally. These would include such functions as accounting and bookkeeping, computer services, purchasing, marketing, advertising, recruiting and training, personnel, payroll and benefits management.

These services would be "sold" to the branches, providing additional revenues for the hub as well as cost savings for the branches.

Personnel and human resources services likely will be outsourced to a Professional Employer Organization (PEO) to provide even greater economies of scale.

Larger "megabrokerage" operations will continue to develop into regional franchisers, licensing firms in surrounding counties—and even states—to use their name, and serving as the "hub" services provider for these satellite firms. When such regional franchises reach critical mass, with perhaps two or three dozen satellite firms under contract, it is conceivable that they will create their own PEO to provide complete human resources, payroll, accounting and temporary services for both hub and satellite firms.

Development of local and regional Internet services and central server technology will also be a function of the hub company, providing both customer access programs and internal communications systems linking all satellite offices. Agent technology training will also be a function of the hub.

The "hub and spoke" concept also facilitates the development of ancillary services—everything from those directly related to the home purchase/sale process, to a variety of services utilized by the homeowner long after the real estate transaction has been concluded. Service providers (warranties, inspections, home security systems, etc.) will find greater value in affiliating with a real estate company that reaches the expanded customer base of the hub and spoke configuration, and will be more willing to establish special pricing and rebates as well as to pay advertising and promotional fees back to the hub company.

ALLIANCES

Both the demand for "one-stop" shopping and the drive toward profitability will require that those who make their living in the real estate business be connected closely with those providing other services that come into play in the real estate transaction.

In some instances, the real estate company may own sister companies that provide certain related services. In other cases, these services will be provided through a structured relationship, which may or may not involve some degree of common ownership.

This will be necessary both to assure prompt and reasonably priced delivery of all those services, and to create a marketing synergy whereby the combined service vendors—the real estate practitioner along with all the rest of the "team"—enjoy a greater volume of business through mutual referral of clients than they would have operating independently.

The larger companies will combine a variety of such ancillary services within owned-and-operated business units. Smaller companies will have contractual relationships with service providers who will either pay a commission on all business generated through the contacts of the real estate company, or who will lease space within the real estate company, or provide "soft money" by jointly sponsoring advertising and promotional campaigns, public relations programs, community service events and/or consumer seminars to develop additional business opportunities.

Competitive forces, including Internet full-service providers, will demand that all services offered in conjunction with the basic real estate transaction either be offered at a discount or have some additional value-added benefits—or, preferably, both. One of the principal value-added benefits for those who obtain the entire package of services through the real estate company will be the high-touch accountability factor that the real estate company and agent will offer to its "customers for life." It is the "Nordstrom effect" creating the "total customer experience" that will be perceived as valuable by the customer of tomorrow.

THE MOM-AND-POP SHOP

Will the individual licensee, operating as a single-person (or husband-wife) shop remain viable?

Probably so, but with limited application. Parallels exist in the medical and legal professions, where individual licensees choose to operate independently. However, there is a great deal of referring that goes on in such instances where specific specialties or levels of expertise are required, or where the case load will simply not permit taking on additional clientele.

One of the drawbacks to such "lone ranger" types of real estate operations will be the consumer's desire to have true one-stop shopping and the perceived need on the part of the consumer to have twenty-four-hour access to information and assistance.

The one-man shop can provide this, but with great difficulty and with diminishing levels of profitability and, equally if not more important, diminishing comfort levels, as the broker-owners will be married to their practices much as the dairy farmer needs to stay close to his cows!

The attraction of going to work for the large national corporation or forming a partnership with other professionals will be too strong for most of the mom-and-pops to resist.

The very small companies will more likely not become involved in mergers or acquisitions, unless their specific niche or market share—or some specific specialty of the owners—is of particular interest to a larger company in filling out its portfolio of business.

It is possible that a new franchise opportunity may develop to provide assistance to the small, independent entrepreneur in establishing connections with related service providers, negotiating volume discounts for clients, providing lead generation and customer management services and handling such functions as accounting, settlement services, and owner benefits such as health care and retirement plans.

ENTER: THE ROLL-UP

It is also possible that some form of "roll-up" activity will take place as a result of all the merger and acquisition activity among the major national players. This will be in response either to the opportunity to grow regionally and eventually be acquired by a national giant, or to the threat of being dwarfed in a marketplace dominated by the giants.

The basic concept of a roll-up is really quite simple: Start with a number of smaller companies, each doing well in its own right, but all hampered by size constraints. There would be a greater degree of efficiency and cost effectiveness in offering a wide variety of consumer services if a number of smaller companies were to be rolled up into a single company. Considerable cost savings can also be created by eliminating duplicated functions and personnel and by the bargaining power (purchasing, advertising, benefits, etc.) that comes with size.

Groups of smaller companies would become roll-up targets in each metropolitan area. They will typically be small to medium-size companies, each with a good reputation and business history. The price offered for each will be based on a business appraisal, using standard formulas which address such issues as number of agents, number of transactions closed in the previous period (one year, two years), number of pending transactions, etc.

The purchase price will be a combination of cash and shares of stock in the new corporation resulting from the roll-up. The purchase of each company will be contingent upon being able to assemble the required number of companies in each location, and perhaps even to the successful launch of a public offering.

If the goals cannot be accomplished within the specified time period, the deal is off and the independent ownership of each company remains in place without change. If the goals are met, the local companies in each metro area are converted to the new name, new image and new ownership immediately, and the general public sees the birth of a new major regional or national force in real estate.

The obstacles to such a venture are many and most of them rather obvious.

First of all, there is the difficult task of pinpointing the companies in each metro area whose market coverage would combine well without too much overlap. Then there are company cultures and the egos of entrepreneurial principals to contend with. (Although the economics of the industry over the past several years—and the changes that we are predicting for the next several—will go a long way to defuse that problem, as more and more owners of small to medium sized companies are seeing the handwriting on the wall and looking for an exit ramp!)

There are also some obvious advantages: First, there are the obvious economies of scale, primarily the elimination of many duplicated functions and personnel as well as the ability to deal in much larger volumes, develop affinity partner relationships with other service providers and support comprehensive programs for lead development and customer follow-up.

From the management viewpoint, a number of new positions and opportunities emerge on the regional and national level. A broker-owner who is adept at recruiting and training, or marketing, advertising or public relations can now apply those skills on a much grander scale, within a much larger region, or perhaps even on a national or international level.

Some of the existing owners and management personnel may be content to continue doing what they have been doing—either within the office or group of offices which they previously owned or managed, or for the expanded regional company. Some may just want out of management and long to go back to listing and selling. Others may want to retire altogether from the business. A successful roll-up will help them all achieve their long and short-term goals.

Another advantage of the roll-up is the geographic diversity that is created.

Prior to the roll-up, each company was dependent largely on the local economy, and its profitability went with the ebb and flow of the local marketplace. In the roll-up, there is some insulation from this roller coaster ride, as the overall health of the national or global economy would provide stability for the entire company even though performance in a specific area may be reduced due to a local or regional economic downturn. The broad national or even global base of the rolled-up entity provides some insulation.

One of the main advantages, at least for the principals of the companies acquired in the roll-up, is the liquidity of the equity. While each owner will receive a certain percentage of the business value in cash at the closing of the transaction, a larger portion will be taken as shares of stock in the rolled-up entity. Assuming that the price established for each company is a true reflection of its worth and that the rolled up entities are able to operate more efficiently and effectively after the roll-up, share values should appreciate—and the liquidity of publicly traded stock will allow owners to either retain their investment, to cash in all or part as lifestyle and retirement needs demand, or to transmit the equity to heirs.

One of the key elements of a successful roll-up will be the fact that the merged entities will operate differently than they had in the past, both with regard to merged departments and functions and in the day-to-day operations—everything from how they recruit, who they are able to attract, how they structure their employment agreements, job descriptions and management responsibilities.

Not only will the size and strength of the new entity be more attractive, but employees and sales personnel will have to perceive definite benefits in working within these larger entities. Just putting a bunch of companies together and then having them all operate as they had in the past will not cut it.

AGENT PARTNERSHIPS

Going to the opposite extreme, there is another structure which may emerge—almost the antithesis of the roll-up or large nationally owned company.

Unlike the roll-up, where broker-owners decide to merge, this new structure will be the result of individual top producing sales agents deciding to create partnerships, patterned somewhat after those commonly created by attorneys or medical professionals.

There are a number of factors that point toward this happening.

First, a number of today's top producers are already immersed in managing their own "business within the business." They are investing a considerable amount of their gross receipts back into their businesses. They are also spending a certain amount of their time managing their little business empires. They are financially successful, at least for the short term, but many have not done a very good job of sheltering their earnings. Relatively few have established a sound retirement program, often living from commission to commission just like their not-so-successful peers—only on a grander scale.

Consider also the changing role of the real estate licensee (see Chapter Three) and the changing demands of the consumer (see Chapter Two). The real estate agent of the future will be required to have highly specialized and diversified skills, particularly in the area of appraisal, negotiation and financial counseling. His/her most valuable hours will be those spent in practicing those skills.

A great many top professionals are also quite good at "mentoring"—teaching others the skills which they have acquired throughout their careers. It was not uncommon in the latter years of the '90s for top agents to earn sizable incomes from mentoring or being personal coaches to others who wanted to follow in their footsteps. And these were not necessarily new-comers to the business. Rather, they were agents who had already achieved some degree of success and who were ready to move to the higher, more rarefied atmosphere of the multimillion dollar producers.

All this sets the stage for yet another form of business practice: the Limited Liability Partnership (LLP) or Limited Liability Corporation (LLC)—business formats that have become almost standards with other professionals, such as doctors and attorneys.

In the LLP, a group of successful top producers, all with their own following (from unlicensed assistants up through the ranks of seasoned professionals who are being mentored), will form a business unit within which they will operate as broker-owners.

As with professional medical groups, the real estate LLP may choose to go into a number of related businesses itself, or to purchase interest in other related businesses which would become part of this full-service real estate center.

The LLP may opt to own the building in which its own real estate activities will be housed and in which a number of related services will also lease space—insurance, appraisal, mortgage, title, settlement services, attorneys, CPAs, property management, builders, developers, etc.: the full-service concept. Perhaps other non-real-estate services which create traffic would also be included, such as a deli or coffee shop, a copy center or a bank branch. Things that will not only generate lease revenue but will also generate a volume of traffic of would-be real estate clients.

Consider the way doctors have formed such partnerships to own medical office buildings, laboratories, diagnostic services, etc. Or the way large law firms have grown up, with a number of founding partners, usually each with his/her own area(s) of expertise, a larger number of junior partners, attorneys who are working their way toward partnership, paralegals, secretaries, information systems managers, etc.

Ditto this form of entrepreneurial activity in the real estate industry of the future.

As with a medical or law practice, the partners will each be responsible for bringing business into the firm. Much of their time will be spent in developing solid contacts within the business community from which real estate business will flow.

Each will have his or her own area of specialization. One may be focused on the high-end properties—the country-club or jet set clientele. Another may be focused on investment properties—and, as a result, have a second area of specialization: property management. First-time buyers (many of whom will be found within the rental units being managed) may provide another specialty. Another may be focused on the senior marketplace. Yet another may be working with corporate, government and military relocation, or specializing with specific immigrant populations.

One partner may be very good at recruiting and training agents. Another's specialty may be developing advertising, marketing and public relations programs. Another may be inclined to handle much of the management of the business itself.

Each will continue to bring in business, but how that business is handled may be quite different from what we have been used to in traditional practice.

In some instances, the partner will handle the

transaction. More often, once initiated, the work will be handed off to others within the firm—either another partner whose area of specialization or whose schedule and work load better matches the task at hand, or perhaps a junior partner or sales licensees who need to build their clientele and experience.

In some instances, a number of the broker-partners and/or junior partners and sales licensees may work as a team on a specific project (e.g. working with a builder or developer client or on a complex multi-party transaction)—just as several attorneys may team up to handle a difficult case.

There will be a number of levels of experience within the firm, and a number of roles specifically involving non-sales functions. Some will be purely clerical and administrative. Others will involve some familiarity with the ins and outs of the real estate transaction and may even require that the practitioners involved be licensed (similar to the paralegal status).

Career paths will be clearly established, with employment agreements spelling out levels of advancement that must be reached within specific periods of time. Training and mentoring programs will be provided for each position and at each level of advancement within firm, from neophyte to senior partner—and all steps in between.

This configuration will lend itself to an all-salaried compensation structure (see Chapter Seven), with increases based on advancement and incentive bonuses based on a combination of individual department (or "team") performance or that of the entire company. The bonus structure will be bottom line (profit) oriented rather than top line (production) oriented.

Chapter 5:

Customer for Life

Much has been written about client follow up—and many dollars spent in its pursuit. We are all aware of the fact that it takes a great deal of time, effort and dollars to cultivate new clients. Repeat business is less expensive to generate than new business. Former clients can provide a great source of new business through personal referrals.

All this is still true. However, most would also agree that even under the best of circumstances, we have the opportunity to generate additional income directly from past clients only every seven to ten years—when they are ready to buy or sell again. There has to be a real estate need before our services can kick in. That is because we see ourselves as "real estate salespeople" and we limit our service offerings to those directly related to the purchase and sale of real estate.

Think about it. We have earned the trust and confidence in our clients who rely on us to counsel and assist them with what are generally the largest purchases of their lifetime. The result of the purchase/sale transaction can have a marked effect on their overall financial success. Was the price right? Were the terms well suited to the specific needs of the client? Was this purchase or sale a wise decision, judged in terms of the client's long-term goals and objectives?

We need to see ourselves more in the role of counselors and facilitators—and perhaps even financial counselors—rather than as just "salespersons."

At the time of the purchase, for example, what other services are needed, not only to bring the transaction to a successful conclusion, but also to assure a seamless transition from one home to the next?

Financing should be right at the top of the list. This is an area in which the average home buyer has little knowledge, yet it is one that the average real estate agent tends to shy away from. Yes, there is a mountain of information available on the Internet today. And there are dozens of Web sites where the buyer can not only get information, but actually complete the loan application process. But does this mean that consumers will have an easier time finding the mortgage that best suits their needs? Quite the contrary. Because there are now so very many options, the decision becomes even more complex. Mortgage counseling is an area in which tomorrow's real estate professional can set herself apart from the crowd and demonstrate truly professional capabilities.

But will the mortgage product that is best for the buyer today necessarily remain the best option throughout his or her term of ownership? A change could be in order due to a dramatic shift in the marketplace—either dropping rates or the appearance on the scene of a more suitable product. Refinancing at the right time can further add to the financial success of the transaction. A change in the client's own needs could signal an opportunity to use financing to achieve yet other goals. Is it time to look at investing in other property? Perhaps selecting a vacation or resort property that might later become a retirement destination? Equity built up in one's primary residence can often be tapped to create such a new investment opportunity. Are there other investment opportunities—not restricted to real estate—that could become a reality by creatively tapping home equity buildup?

Traditionally, as an industry, we have not taken a proactive role in driving the resale marketplace. Rather, we have reacted whenever a consumer has expressed an interest in buying or selling.

A REAL INVESTMENT—OR JUST SHELTER?

I cringe whenever I hear a real estate professional (broker or agent) say that given today's economic landscape, we should see the home as shelter, but no longer as investment. While this may be true in many cases, it may well be because we, as an industry, have not treated the home purchase as an investment, but have focused instead on the shelter/lifestyle side of the equation. We have taken a "transactional" approach to our business, focusing on the consumer as "buyer" or "seller" rather than as "homeowner" and "customer for life."

It goes without saying that if someone had purchased an insurance policy, a certificate of deposit, an annuity, bonds or a portfolio of stock ten years ago and not looked at it again—never checking its performance, doing nothing to improve it or leverage it any further—it would probably not be a very good investment today. And if that "investor" did not analyze the initial investment very carefully and did not weigh its advantages in light of a number of other factors, including alternate investment opportunities and his or her own financial position at the time of the investment, it may not have been a good investment to begin with.

Likewise with the purchase of a home. If the real estate agent simply recommended a mortgage company—or two or three—and the buyer selected one of them at random and applied for a loan, accepting whichever loan product at whatever rate and terms offered, there is somewhat of a chance that he or she did not start out that cycle of ownership on the best financial footing. Compounding the problem, that homeowner probably settled in and did nothing more than make the payments for five, or seven or more years, and made no changes until he or she decided for whatever reasons that it was time to get back into the market and look for another home.

No question that the home provided shelter. There are perhaps some questions about its delivery on the lifestyle side of the equation—unless the home and neighborhood provided everything that the homeowner wanted and that his money could buy. Most probably there are questions about the home's value as an investment—at least in light of the performance of other investments of similar amounts over the same period of time.

The experience is further diminished if the homeowner eventually decides to sell again and falls into the grip of an inexperienced or less-than-competent listing agent whose *modus operandi* is to take the listing as low as he can get it, put it into the MLS and hope someone sells it. Then, if all else fails, get a price reduction to bring a buyer to the closing table.

Let's do a little "What Iffing":

What if the real estate company had that buyer pre-approved immediately, before a home was selected for purchase? And what if, in the approval process, the buyer were counseled professionally on a variety of loan products available, weighing each one against the homeowner's present and likely short-term future economic position? And what if, based on that counseling, the homeowner selected the very best available loan product for his or her immediate and short-term needs?

Just as there is more to negotiate than just price when buying a home, there is more to consider than just the interest rate when making a loan. Much more.

The agent who is financing savvy will evaluate the length of time that the buyer is planning to live in the home. If another move is anticipated in a relatively short period of time, an adjustable rate might be a good choice. If the buyer anticipates increasing income levels over the next two or three years, a seller buy-down might be in order.

Now, not to get hung up on this one point, but real estate agents who are skilled in financing will understand that with a buy-down, the buyer can actually qualify for a much more expensive home based on the initial bought-down rate. Rather than negotiate a few thousand off the asking price, a full-price offer with the seller paying the same few thousand dollars to buy down the loan for the first one, two or three years, could be beneficial to both buyer and seller. Similarly, when representing the seller, a seller's buy-down, rather than a price reduction, can open the listing up to a much larger number of qualified buyers and give the listing a real competitive advantage over other similarly priced homes.

But it takes an agent who is fully cognizant of the financing process and who really wants to go the extra mile to establish a *customer for life* rather than just a client for a single transaction.

In a company that has created areas of specialization, financial counseling may be done by someone other than the buyer's (or seller's) agent. In this scenario, the financial counselor may become involved even further in the client's personal investment picture. Where are the limits on service capabilities within a full-service "one-stop-shopping" operation? If the customer is willing to put his or her trust in the real estate company to handle all the details regarding the initial purchase, then why not purchase other financial services from the same company?

That is precisely the *Customer for Life* concept.

Let's take the "What If" exercise a step further:

What if each buyer (now *customer for life*) received an "annual review" from the real estate company, detailing such things as:

Calculation of homeowners current equity based on mortgage balance (from original loan documents, assuming payments made according to schedule and no refinancing has occurred) and appreciation factors (based on resale statistics for comparable homes in the same neighborhood).

Qualification to eliminate PMI due to buildup of equity (by both appreciation and principal payoff) beyond the twenty-percent minimum required by lenders.

Calculation of potential savings by refinancing at the current time, considering the rate and terms of the initial loan, current refinancing rates and fees as well as any new mortgage products which may have become available since the original mortgage was taken out and which might be more suitable to the owner's current status.

Expiration and renewal options for original home warranty.

If the company is also in the insurance business, information on applicable insurance rates and coverages could also be referenced.

And what if the agent or some other "specialist" from the company personally contacted that homeowner after the "annual review" had been prepared, and set an appointment to review it? (Just as an insurance company or stock broker might do.)

In order to accomplish this with some degree of sophistication and without a great amount of labor, some system would have to be established to track both the individual purchaser ("customer") as well as the overall real estate activity in the neighborhood. Current mortgage rates and products would also have to be tracked and interrelated with the data on customers and properties.

Fortunately, all of this is already being tracked. Programming to interrelate all the data would need to be devised. (Could this be a potential new role for the MLS? With listing data no longer the private domain of the MLS, perhaps computerized customer and property sales tracking could be a service provided to all member firms?)

And real estate professionals—either full-service agents or specialists assigned to the task—would have to be trained to interpret the data and provide the counseling service. In companies with in-house mortgage services or affinity relationships with lenders, employees from the mortgage side may be utilized to provide this information directly to the homeowner or to prepare all necessary information for presentation by the real estate professional placed in charge of that *customer for life*.

Carry this a step further. Another "What If":

What if every time a new buyer client was interviewed, and his or her needs and wants identified, that information was matched automatically with data on previous buyers (*customers for life*) who had been in their current homes for a specific period of time— say three years or more. (Note that we are not recommending that the average period of homeownership, currently around seven to eight years, be used as the benchmark. This system, if properly utilized, should be a means of reducing the average period of time between purchases by making homeowners aware of new opportunities rather than waiting for them to think about making a change in homeownership.)

Existing homeowners whose properties matched the needs and wants of the new buyer client would be contacted with a message similar to the following on a personalized memo or letter:

It is our policy to inform our customers whenever we identify a buyer who is interested in a property similar to theirs. We have just begun working with a buyer whose interests match your property description and who would be financially qualified to purchase your home, based on our most recent market analysis. If you are thinking about selling, or if you would be interested in discussing your home's current market value, and other properties that might be suited to your current needs and lifestyle, please give us a call.
Your home provides shelter, lifestyle and a financial investment. We are committed to helping our clients and customers realize the best values in all three areas during a lifetime of ownership.

Some may opt to send the notification by mail or e-mail and then follow up by phone. Others may choose to call the homeowner directly, creating an even greater sense of urgency. Where some interest is expressed, an offer can be extended to set an appointment for the potential buyer to tour their home. This establishes the legitimacy of the contact—as opposed to the old "we may have a buyer for your home" routine commonly used with FSBOs.

Along with the analysis of the annual review document, the company would determine changing needs of the homeowner. Expanding or contracting family size, job and salary advancements may signal a change in lifestyle or investment potential. Changes in the surrounding neighborhood, highways, commute patterns, etc. may indicate a move might be in order. If the company has relationships with builders and developers, new construction may be enticing.

In the worst-case scenario, the customer has no interest in moving in the near future, but may be quite happy to see how their investment has appreciated and that the real estate company is keeping them informed.

The "annual review" provides the basis for a customer follow-up program that both maintains contact with previous buyers (call them *customers for life*) and provides a proactive means of driving the market—either to create move-up activity or to develop and maintain customer loyalty, personal referrals and eventual repeat business.

Traditional client follow-up programs have generally focused on keeping the real estate agent's name in front of the client after the transaction has been completed in order to remind them to refer other potential clients and to try to stay in touch long enough that they contact the same agent when it is once again time to sell.

Such programs have had a limited measure of success, particularly for that very small percentage of agents who use such programs diligently and maintain unending personal contact with their clients. But, for the most part, such follow-up programs will be more or less futile in the future, and for several reasons:

First, the consumer is already overwhelmed by mailboxes (and now e-mail boxes) stuffed with similar pleas for attention. Telemarketing, both personal and automated, has reached such epidemic proportions that one of the hottest selling new pieces of telephone technology is caller ID—and new call-blocking systems that reject all calls from anonymous sources.

Further, the consumer of today does not want to know how good the real estate agent is, how many transactions he or she has been involved in, and is not at all concerned about the fact that we "really want his business." The consumer of today wants information—useful information—something that will make his or her life happier, easier; something that will help save money or make money; something that will help solve a problem or create an opportunity (for the consumer, not for the real estate agent).

All those "Hey, remember me? I'm your real estate agent!" messages will go into the circular file or be relegated to some vast cyberspace wastebasket.

To get their attention, you will have to give them information that they want and can use. And to get their business, you will have to show them why it is in their best interests to do something. (Inertia is the strongest force keeping homeowners from becoming buyers or sellers.) And, once convinced that doing some business is a good idea, the only remaining step is to convince them that they can do that business best—most easily, most quickly and most successfully—with you.

The agent of tomorrow will still have to sell his/her own professionalism, but will have to do it by demonstration rather than by proclamation. While the customer of today asks "What have you done for me lately?" The customer of tomorrow will ask "What can you do for me right now?" And those who can consistently provide a positive answer to that question will be the big winners.

Financing will remain one of the most important elements in the real estate transaction, and those who know how to advise and counsel effectively in all of the financial aspects of homeownership will earn the consumer's respect as the professionals who can make their home owning experience successful.

ONE-STOP SHOPPING

Where the real estate company has assembled a number of products and services related to the process of homeownership, the ultimate value of the *customer for life* will extend beyond the commissions made on each listing or sale. That is one of the motivations driving some of the big national companies that have decided to enter the residential real estate business.

Take MidAmerican Energy Holdings, for example. This Midwestern utilities company set its sights on the real estate industry as an attempt to gain access to the homeowner who would also be the customer for gas and electric utility service once deregulation would give the consumer choices in the selection of suppliers.

The company's approach was to purchase real estate companies that had significant market share and that were well established and well managed entities. (At this writing, the company has 146 offices in eleven states and is the second-largest independent residential real estate brokerage operation in the United States.)

MidAmerican then added additional product line to generate further profits from each customer contact, including mortgage origination, closing administrative services and title abstracting. Through affinity relationships with third parties, the company also provides referrals for other pre-closing and post-closing services such as home warranty, home inspection, home security, property and casualty insurance, home maintenance and home repair, and is developing various related e-commerce services.

MidAmerican has since put its residential real estate operations into a subsidiary, Home-Services.Com, Inc., which successfully launched an initial public offering in October, 1999. Shortly thereafter, an investor group led by Warren Buffett's Berkshire Hathaway, Inc. reached a definitive agreement to purchase MidAmerican Energy Holdings. The concept seems to be attracting some savvy investors!

For the consumer, this model represents the convenience (and perhaps costs savings) of one-stop shopping. For the company, it is similar to the "superstore" retailing concept: Put a multitude of products in front of each customer rather than sell only one product.

For the real estate company and/or agent who is strategizing for future success, putting the customer at the center of the transaction is more than just a platitude—it is the key concept that will unlock a whole new world of opportunity.

Chapter 6:

Niche Marketing

The consumer base is becoming more diverse, and an increasing number of "niche" marketing opportunities are unfolding, particularly as communications breakthroughs provide new avenues for targeting our message to specific market niches.

While some new companies may be formed specifically to address certain market niches, in most cases the opportunity will be seized by existing real estate companies creating separate "divisions" focused on those niches.

Or, absent the initiative on the part of the company, individual agents may opt to concentrate on specific niches that are of special interest to them, or that seem to hold out unique business development opportunities.

The mere fact that the unique needs of a specific segment of the marketplace are not being given proper recognition by "mainstream" real estate brokerage operations will make it an attractive target for those who decide to zero in on that market segment.

Widespread access to the Internet is providing a unique new ability to focus advertising and marketing efforts efficiently and effectively on specific market segments. Whereas in a previous era it may not have been cost-effective to utilize available advertising media—newspaper, radio and television—to target small segments of the marketplace, Internet and central server technology now makes such segmenting very efficient, inexpensive and effective.

This will create a whole new focus on niche marketing.

As we outline some of the potential niche markets, it should be noted that some of them are interrelated, in that they require many of the same skill sets and personal and technical resources.

Consider, for example, the first-time buyer, the English-as-a-second-language buyer, and the urban-center buyer. One element common to all three distinct niches is that of financing. In many cases, all three niches will require special knowledge and expertise in the area of financing, and perhaps even special financing instruments tailored to each specific niche customer.

While a certain percentage of first-time buyers may be in higher income categories, the largest segment of the first-time buyer population will be at the lower end of the income spectrum, often requiring special financing and sometimes having to go through a considerable amount of coaching and education in order to make home ownership a reality.

The same can be said of serving the immigrant population and addressing the specific needs and opportunities of the central cities. While a certain segment of that business will involve consumers with a certain measure of affluence, a much larger percentage will be with entry-level buyers.

THE FIRST-TIME BUYER NICHE

Real estate economists point to an increase in first-time buyer activity as one of the trends that will help stabilize the resale marketplace during the opening decades of the twenty-first century.

However, the "first-time buyer" is really a rather artificial category, one that relates to a temporary state of ownership—or lack thereof. Unlike niches such as "the senior marketplace," "the immigrant population," "urban centers" or "Americans with disabilities," there is no actual physical condition, geographic location or demographic category that identifies and defines the people within this niche.

With the increasing tendency to marry later, to have children later, and to create highly mobile lifestyles centered more on career enhancement rather than family development, the first-time buyer segment of the population will include a sizeable percentage of people who have been renting rather than buying, not because of any economic necessity but because of lifestyle preferences. The average first-time buyer will be older, wealthier, more educated and more experienced than in the past.

However, there is an even much larger segment of the population which includes a relatively small number of homeowners but a vast number who are potential first-time buyers. This is the low-to-moderate income population—the folks who have been trapped in a rental mentality, although the money they are spending on monthly rental payments is often more than others are spending on house payments. As a very astute civic leader once put it: "They're already paying for a mortgage—it's just not their own."

This segment of the population has been all but ignored by the real estate industry, mainly because of the disproportion between the amount of work required to move them into ownership compared with the rather meager commissions that accompany that accomplishment.

But it is a segment of the population whose time has come.

Within this population segment we see increasing levels of education and expanding employment opportunities. More social programs are being refocused on this population segment. Loan instruments have been developed specifically for the low to middle income buyer, and many state, county and city programs have been created to provide assistance to buyers in these categories.

Couple this with the fact that the unbundling of real estate services and the subsequent involvement of many other players in the home buying process may tend to bring real estate commissions more in line with the amount of time actually spent on the transaction rather than tied to a percentage of the selling price. This may help "level the playing field," where the half-million dollar sale no longer automatically produces ten times the fee that would be generated by the fifty-thousand dollar transaction. In that scenario, a renewed interest in the first-time buyer marketplace may well emerge.

In evaluating the opportunities in the first-time buyer niche, one should also keep in mind the fact that building a base in the first-time buyer marketplace lays the foundation for additional opportunities. Having a first-time buyer waiting in the wings creates an opportunity for an existing owner of a lower-priced property to enter the move-up market. And many of today's first-time buyers will enter the ranks of the move-up buyer in the not-too-distant future.

Remember the principle of the *Customer for Life*.

LUXURY HOMES

At the other end of the spectrum, new opportunities are also unfolding for those who select the luxury home market as their specific niche.

Potential buyers and sellers in the high end market frequently are dispersed over a wide geographic area—sometimes even globally.

Prior to the advent of the Internet, reaching the high-end buyer and seller was difficult, and marketing efforts expensive and time consuming.

With today's 360-degree "virtual home tour" capabilities, luxury home Web sites make these listings accessible to buyers and investors worldwide.

Establishing a position within the luxury home marketing niche will also provide the basis for affinity marketing programs with suppliers of products and services geared to the high-end buyer. Revenues could be derived from affinity relationships, either by way of advertising fees for inclusion on the Web site, or by royalties, finders fees or commissions paid on all transactions resulting from the affinity relationship.

Whether emerging opportunities for tapping the luxury home marketplace are captured by the real estate industry or by outside industries who will charge the real estate players "referral" fees for this business is yet to be determined. One thing is certain, however: This market niche holds too much promise to be overlooked.

THE IMMIGRANT MARKETPLACE

One of the demographic trends that economists point to as bolstering the residential real estate marketplace of the future is the increasing influx of an immigrant population—many of whom are ready and able to enter the ranks of homeownership.

Some of the real estate agents who will take a commanding position in these emerging market niches will come from that immigrant population itself, as enterprising newcomers get established and take advantage of the opportunity to become licensed for the specific purpose of providing real estate services to their fellow immigrants.

Some forward-looking real estate companies are already establishing separate divisions just to handle marketing to specific ethnic groups settling in their market area.

Such an operation would identify key leaders in the immigrant community and, through them, establish programs to help educate the immigrant population on the advantages of home ownership and to coach them through the process. Along the way, enterprising men and women would be recruited into the industry, with the real estate company sponsoring their real estate education and licensing. These agents would serve as the nucleus of the new division, developing marketing materials in their own language and distributing these materials throughout the local immigrant population.

The company would probably establish some form of cooperative marketing and communications programs in conjunction with other merchants and professionals who are wanting to establish inroads into these growing ethnic population centers. These "partners" would pay for advertising in brochures distributed by the real estate company. The real estate company would also distribute its marketing materials through local merchants catering to that specific ethnic population.

In conjunction with civic and community agencies and local educational resources, these niche market divisions could create informational brochures, and bilingual forms, contracts and legal documents for use with the immigrant population. (In current practice, standard English-language documents are often utilized in transactions involving non-English-speaking buyers and sellers, generating confusion and distrust and requiring the services of an interpreter, often an attorney fluent in both languages.)

Public relations opportunities will abound for niche marketers who develop programs and services specifically geared to helping the immigrant population.

A NICHE FOR THE DISABLED

From a real estate perspective, the term "disability" often conjures up thoughts about such things as adding wheelchair ramps, building wheelchair accessible facilities or providing braille symbols on elevator panels. Besides the inconveniences often experienced in dealing with day-to-day accommodations, those with disabilities may also encounter unique difficulties in the process of acquiring or disposing of property.

One Pacific Northwest real estate company (Tomlinson Black, in Spokane, Wash.) discovered the opportunities in niche marketing quite accidentally when a blind couple interviewed for jobs with the company. This husband-and-wife team went on to develop a strong marketing niche for the company within the blind community and lead the company to explore similar opportunities with other types of disabilities.

Inspired by the success of this first team, the company established inroads into a variety of disabled niches within the local community, The game plan always involved first hiring someone with a specific disability and then, utilizing that person's knowledge, expertise and contacts, establishing marketing and educational programs to provide real estate assistance for others with the same disabilities.

Such programs will not only generate untold goodwill within the community, but will also create a loyal clientele, not only with the disabled, but with their family members and all who are connected in any way with servicing their needs. The circles of influence that evolve from such programs provide almost unlimited opportunities for the real estate company and/or agent focusing on those market niches.

THE GRAYING OF AMERICA

Every seven and one-half seconds, a new fifty-year-old emerges on the demographic charts. This trend is expected to continue into the twenty-first century. By the year 2010, one in every five Americans will be over age sixty-five.

Seniors are already the largest single group of property owners in the nation, yet traditional real estate marketing programs are often targeted to the "twenty-five to forty-nine-year-old" population. Not only has the length of life for the senior citizen been extended, but the quality of life has also vastly improved with seniors remaining healthier much longer and having the financial resources to enjoy during their retirement.

While the income of the senior marketplace may be declining relative to the increasing incomes of the younger set, the net worth of this segment of the population remains very high. According to the U.S. Commerce Department, the average household wealth of the sixty-five to seventy-four-year-old population is over $100,000.

The trend toward early retirement has also spawned a "second career" syndrome, with many second-career retirees remaining in the workplace even beyond the traditional retirement age of sixty-five.

There is a real estate component in almost every senior citizen's retirement planning. More than eighty percent of the senior population are homeowners and only about twenty percent of them are still paying on a mortgage. For the vast majority there is an existing home that has become too large, too old or too unsuited to the physical and/or financial needs of the senior.

Perhaps the location is wrong: Minneapolis, where the temperatures plummet, rather than sun-drenched Phoenix; or Kansas City, but the grandchildren are in Seattle; or Parsippany where the corporate retiree last relocated, but his origins (and heart) are still in St. Louis.

In recent years, as retirees tend to be younger, and seniors decidedly more active, there has been a noticeable trend among the retiree marketplace to want to have access to cultural and intellectual (and even physical) pursuits. Developers are beginning to target college towns for retirement communities.

And the information age has not left the seniors behind. The over-fifty-five age group is one of the most rapidly expanding user populations on the Internet. Perhaps this is because they simply have more time, and perhaps they have discovered that it is an economical way to communicate with grown children and grandchildren scattered around the world. Easy chair e-commerce will likely find an increasing customer base among this segment of the population.

For all these reasons, targeting the senior marketplace would seem a natural for the real estate company and agent of the future.

And don't forget the relationship marketing that is inherent in this segment of the business. Providing services specifically tailored to the senior marketplace can help establish business relationships with a much wider market segment: the children, grandchildren and others who are concerned about and/or responsible for the well-being of these aging citizens.

One of the best things about developing this market niche is that people in this age group generally have more time on their hands and are often looking for a little supplemental income. These resources can be tapped to put together marketing programs and to get the word out about your services among a variety of senior groups.

Interest in the senior marketplace could also begin with retirement planning among a much younger market segment. As benefits programs become increasingly more expensive, employers will look for ways to provide programs for their employees at little or no expense.

Tailoring a "real estate and retirement" program for delivery to groups of employees within local businesses could provide access to an ongoing stream of business from those sources. Such programs can be joint ventures involving not only the local real estate company or agent, but also other service providers wishing to reach this marketplace. Included might be health care providers, insurers, investment advisors and financial planners. Each would provide a segment of the program, and all would share jointly the costs of promotion and delivery of the program.

THE RETURN TO URBAN CENTERS

During the latter half of the twentieth century, the flight to the suburbs left many central cities in a state of semi-abandonment and decay.

Once predominantly owner-occupied neighborhoods quickly changed to rental properties of diminished economic value. Absentee landlords had milked
them for whatever rents could be obtained, spending
little money maintaining them.

Many of those who stayed in the cities were older
homeowners who were either reluctant to leave behind the neighborhoods in which they had lived and
raised their families, or for whom the relocation to more
expensive suburban property was not economically
possible. They watched their neighborhoods and their
properties decline, as the downward spiral created
slums where there had been thriving neighborhoods;
hovels where there had been homes—and left the core
cities bereft of the care and pride of ownership once
associated with neighborhoods having a predominance
of owner-occupied real estate.

Along with the homeowner exodus came the
demise of the commercial and professional businesses
that both supported and were supported by that population.

At the turn of the millennium, however,
America's attention seems to be refocusing on the importance of the central city as the hub around which
suburban growth needs to be re-centered. Someone
wisely noted, "You can't be a suburb of nothing."

Within our urban centers, there are countless
new real estate opportunities ready to be reaped by
niche marketers who learn to cultivate that business.
The demise of urban school systems once seemed to be
a stumbling block to residential real estate in the cities, as the twenty-five to forty-nine-year old age group
was made up largely of families with school-age chil-

dren. Today many young professionals who have not yet started families are expressing interest in city living.

There is a new revival of interest in the kinds of space that older buildings can provide. "Loft" districts—blocks of warehousing and manufacturing buildings that have been converted into spacious apartments and condos—are developing in many of America's older inner cities. Entertainment, shopping and sports arenas are returning to urban centers, and along with them, a host of other businesses and services—all very attractive to the young professional set.

In the City of St. Louis, for example, acres of public housing are currently yielding to the wrecking ball. Tracts of land once amassed for these projects are being turned back into normal street grid patterns. High-rise structures which housed public welfare occupants will give way to single family homes and condominiums— the vast majority geared to market rate sales (not rental properties), but with a reasonable mix of low to moderate income housing (still single-family detached and condominiums) which will be developed and sold with some governmental subsidies.

In Boston, the massive mansions built during the latter half of the nineteenth century were turned into apartments, offices and rooming houses when the Great Depression hit. During the past year, there has been a resurgence in the urban marketplace and those stately old structures are now commanding top dollar from wealthy professionals who want the convenience of urban living without sacrificing the space they experienced in the suburbs.

This return to homes in the urban centers contradicts all previous long-term economic forecasts and "conventional wisdom" which said that these large structures would be more valuable carved up into condominiums or revamped into office and commercial space. Could it be that it is more than just economics that drives the marketplace—that consumers may have wants and needs that our educated "real estate sense" tends to ignore or place little value on?

A recent *Wall Street Journal* article on the resurgence of city properties in Boston quotes a buyer who had been living on a forty-six-acre horse farm in New Jersey and who wanted to return to city life. Charmed by Boston's neighborhoods, he purchased two apartment buildings in Beacon Hill, turning them into single-family homes—including one for himself. His rationale, as quoted in *The Journal*: "What people want out of their living style is not to spend so much time doing things like mowing the lawn, painting the house." "There was a time for that," he says of his farmhouse days. "I love this town and I work downstairs."

THE LOW TO MODERATE INCOME BUYER

In contrast to this upscale market renaissance, another untapped source of business in the cities lies in the lower income population—those who are earning a living, and have income sufficient to support a modest house payment but who do not yet have the personal resources for the required down payment, or who may need counseling in a variety of related areas, such as establishing credit, household budgeting, basic home maintenance skills, etc. before they can enter the ranks of homeowners.

With the re-awakening of interest in the central cities will come a re-awakening of interest on the part of those who understand the potential revenue streams that the revitalization of these long-abandoned wastelands will provide.

The adept urban niche marketer (individual agent or company) will put together a coordinated program involving civic leaders, neighborhood and community resources, mortgage lenders (especially banks in need of meeting Community Reinvestment Act targets) and rental property owners to tap a wealth of hidden commission opportunities within these urban centers. And, in the process, they will be establishing valuable connections upon which to build additional business referrals.

One such program, announced in the spring of 1999, involved a "partnership" between two unlikely entities, Cendant Mortgage, ranked the tenth-largest lender in the United States, and the Philadelphia NAACP. Known as the "Next Generation Mortgage Program," this ground-breaking relationship was designed to help first-time buyers achieve their dream of homeownership and to help increase the percentage of homeowners within the City of Philadelphia. The program not only provides an annual $6 million loan commitment for the city, but also special mortgage programs requiring no down payment and no private mortgage insurance as well as an array of educational programs designed to counsel potential buyers on mortgage and credit issues.

Finding the properties suitable for the lower-income first-time-buyer marketplace will also be a challenge—and a significant opportunity for agents or companies who succeed. Many of the properties that would suit the financial ability of many first-time buyers are currently under the control of landlords who see these properties as significant investment opportunities. Meanwhile, city authorities have been using the pressure of building code enforcement and occupancy permit requirements to strong-arm landlords into compliance. Perhaps it is time to address the problems—and the opportunities—from an economic position, developing win-win tactics that will allow investors to reap their rewards while moving a larger percentage of the rental population into home ownership.

It is the unique combination of the renewed interest in city living among the younger upscale market along with the increasing opportunity for ownership among the existing urban rental population that will combine to create real estate opportunities for those who want to specialize in this niche.

Adding to the opportunity is the fact that for the most part real estate companies have abandoned the central cities for the more lucrative commission opportunities in the suburbs. It was easier to sell the $250,000 house in the suburbs than the $60,000 house in the city—and at four times the commission income.

In the future, the trend toward downscaling of commissions coupled with the "unbundling" of the real estate transaction may change all that, particularly as agent compensation becomes more closely tied to the amount of time put into the transaction. As in the legal profession, the real estate practitioners' fees may come to be based more on the actual services performed with no direct relationship to the ultimate selling price.

The renewed focus on urban centers also dove-tails with the increasing need for development of housing for the retirement age owner. Not all retirees envision going out into the desert or treading barefoot on sunny beaches to await their maker. Many will want to be around bustling centers, where there is art, entertainment, restaurants, shows, museums, symphony halls and good shopping—all within walking distance or at the end of a very short taxi ride.

Redeveloping urban centers will provide that environment. The prices will be relatively reasonable (at least at first), considering the advantages, and there will be plenty of cash from the sale of grand suburban homes to support those more modest urban purchases—with perhaps enough left over to add to the investment portfolio.

It is also in the urban centers where much of the "new" real estate activity will be focused: Many immigrant groups will gravitate toward the urban centers, either because that environment is more familiar to them or because of the more reasonable prices.

First-time buyers will also be able to find some real bargains—at least in the beginning—which will increase in value as their earning power also increases—creating a flow of commissions from move-up opportunities for those who are visionary enough to tap into the trends.

Those who are not looking to the cities as we go into the Twenty-first century will likely miss some of the best opportunities this industry has seen—or will see—for a long time.

Chapter 7:

The Demise of the Independent Contractor

For a great many years—perhaps ever since the beginning of the IRS Code—many businesses have steadfastly clung to independent contractor relationships, both to avoid creating any agency relationships that would make the owners responsible for the actions of the independent contractor and to eliminate the expenses, paperwork and red tape associated with having employees, such as federal, state and local withholding deposits, workmen's compensation and unemployment insurance premiums.

Real estate broker-owners have been among the leading proponents of the independent contractor status, and the National Association of Realtors has lobbied very successfully on several occasions when the independent contractor status appeared to be on Congress's endangered species list.

While the independent contractor status helped

real estate brokerage firms avoid a number of direct and indirect costs associated with having employees, they were not as successful in eliminating liability for the actions of their independent contractors, as licensing laws still hold the managing broker and/or broker owner responsible for the actions of the licensees operating under them. So a major advantage usually associated with the independent contractor status was missing within the context of the real estate firm.

On the flip side, the very nature of the independent contractor status requires that the company abdicate almost all control over the actions of its agents. The independent contractor status would be breached if the company required agents to keep a certain schedule, to attend meetings regularly, to observe a certain dress code, etc. Viewed from the perspective of management, the loss of control inherent in the independent contractor status is rather monumental.

In the name of protecting the independent contractor status, the real estate brokerage industry also eschewed programs that might create the appearance of an employee-employer relationship. As a result, many of the things that are typically used to attract and retain employees in other industries have been noticeably absent from the real estate industry, such as health benefits, retirement programs, paid holidays and vacations.

If the real estate industry is going to compete for some of the brightest talent coming through our colleges and universities, a more stable form of income generation may have to be put into place, not to mention the need for benefits and perks not traditionally associated with real estate sales.

As real estate companies grew from "mom and pop" status to "megabroker" proportions, an increasing number of employees became associated with the typical brokerage firm—and with them, all of the paperwork and compliance requirements associated with the employer/employee relationship have already become part of the brokerage management business.

Administrative and clerical staff are generally employees—as are most management personnel.

To further complicate the picture, many of today's top producers are now engaging the services of "personal assistants." In some instances, the employment agreements, payroll, taxes, etc. are left totally to the discretion of the sales agents hiring these assistants. In other instances, the real estate company sets forth certain rules and regulations for the process, sometimes even requiring that the personal assistants be hired by the company and, in effect, "leased back" to the individual agents. This is to provide some assurance that all regulatory requirements are met, paperwork in order and payroll taxes properly handled.

Other companies, worried about the liability for their agents' personal assistants, have set up "firewalls" to shift total responsibility for the existence and actions of personal assistants to the individual agents who hire them. While the concern is real, the solution is somewhat lacking, as licensing laws still hold the broker/owner and/or managing broker responsible for the actions of its licensees. If a consumer—buyer, seller, prospect—is harmed in any way in a transaction because of something that a personal assistant does (or fails to do), or says (or fails to say), it is highly likely that the agent, the assistant(s) and the real estate company will all be named in any legal action that results.

As brokers begin to analyze more carefully the actual cost of hiring, training and retaining sales agents, it becomes more obvious that perhaps the independent contractor status is not all that it has been cracked up to be. In fact, since a number of accounting, payroll and human resources functions are already in place as a result of the increased number of clerical, administrative and managerial employees now associated with the large real estate firm, some of the onus previously associated with having employees has already been eliminated.

SALARIED, COMMISSIONED—OR BOTH?

Raising the issue among groups of experienced broker owners always generates a number of very predictable responses:

"If we were to put our agents on a salary tomorrow, we'd quickly go broke!"

"A salaried structure will take away the incentive of our best agents. It's only the poorer producers who would benefit."

"We'd lose our best agents to the competition if we even suggested putting them on a salary."

The reason for these rather predictable knee-jerk responses lies mainly in the fact that we tend to see changes as isolated pieces of the puzzle, rather than fitting them into the larger picture of massive changes that will be occurring in the industry.

There is little doubt that introducing a salaried structure into a real estate company without changing many other aspects of the management of that company would spell disaster.

It seems equally obvious that putting all of our agents on salary without changing other aspects of the broker/agent relationship—and of the brokerage/consumer relationship—would also be counterproductive.

And if there were no external forces impacting the total structure and future of the brokerage industry, it would not make much sense to even think about altering the agent compensation picture.

In yesterday's world of real estate, where the real estate company was singularly focused on listings, where the agent was the sole source of information and assistance for the home seller or buyer, showing property, holding open houses, and shepherding transactions from contract to settlement, the existing structure seemed to work fine. (The operative word here is "seemed," as the process was actually moving the brokerage firm further and further away from control of both the customer base and its own bottom line.)

However, a great many of the other changes occurring within the consumer marketplace and the world of technology would seem to suggest that the time might be right for rethinking the entire field of agent compensation.

PROS and CONS

Beyond the legal and financial aspects of the employer/employee relationship, there are a number of more personal issues that seem to favor the maintenance of the independent contractor status. The rather unusual amount of independence traditionally associated with real estate sales has been one of the major attractions of this career. As independent contractors, real estate licensees are free to set their own hours, and their income potential is limited only by their ability and willingness to work hard.

There is more perception than reality in this, however, as many eager young licensees have quickly learned. The degree of freedom that one experiences in this business is in almost inverse proportion to the level of earnings achieved. Much of the success that has been achieved by top producers has been the result of their willingness to work not only long hours, but very odd hours, constantly rearranging personal and family schedules to meet the needs, wants or whims of client or prospect.

Many have washed out simply because they were not self disciplined enough to handle the "freedom" of the business—either not putting their shoulder to the wheel and cranking out the business, or, working very hard but not managing their money wisely, and finding themselves unable to discipline themselves to live within a budget that will carry them from commission to commission.

The independent contractor status has also proven a hindrance to effective recruiting on college campuses. Some of the brightest and most promising talent—the key people needed to bring a real estate company into the new millennium-have not been impressed with the prospect of having to work on a "commission only" basis, when other jobs in other industries would offer them reasonable starting salaries and benefits.

Some real estate companies have instituted a

"hiring bonus" structure that would give the promising new recruit some cushion until the first commission is generated. Some now offer a temporary salaried structure to cover the start-up months until regular commission production develops. Others have set up mentoring plans to help move the new recruit more quickly to the first commission check.

One of the problems with the concept of breaking away from the independent contractor status lies with a misunderstanding of the term "employee."

Does *employee* necessarily mean *salaried*?

Yes, and no.

There are many examples in other sales-related industries of compensation structures which involve either a nominal base salary and then a commission schedule based on performance, or a monthly salary as a "draw" against commissions.

From the agent's point of view, there are distinct advantages to the salaried status: a steady base paycheck, and the elimination of the need for computing and making quarterly tax payments (and the elimination of the "big hit" at annual tax time when sufficient quarterly payments were not made!). The "draw" structure also establishes a specific goal that must be met—not just an arbitrary "target".

And from the company's viewpoint there are obvious advantages in having the ability to establish work schedules, assign specific duties, and require attendance at meetings. The company has a much greater degree of control.

Employment contracts can also spell out levels of production that must be attained and levels of compensation—including salary, bonuses and benefits—

commensurate with specific production targets. This would have a positive impact on budgeting and planning.

The drawbacks? The most obvious, from the company's point of view, would seem to be the danger of paying out salaries and benefits to agents who fail to perform. From the agent's point of view, there may be some chafing at the thought of losing some independence—of having to maintain normal office hours, schedule vacation days in advance and generally put up with all the constraints normally associated with a "real job."

Both, however, are not well founded fears, and all but disappear when put to the test of a serious analysis of the business we are in—or are going to be —in the not-too-distant future.

From the management point of view, the notion of hiring a great number of agents with the hopes that they will perform and contribute to the company's bottom line is an ill-founded business practice based on a lack of understanding of the real costs of doing business. Just because we can bring licensees on board without the risk of having to pay a weekly salary, many are lulled into complacency and fail to fully account for what non-producing or under-producing agents really cost.

From the agent's point of view, the key to making a salaried mode work will be the introduction of some "structure" into the workplace, while at the same time providing for a high degree of personal latitude in the performance of the duties assigned to the salaried agent. This will also require the development of a highly structured environment in which a great many of the burdensome tasks currently associated with an agent's performance in the listing, selling scenarios are done efficiently and with a great deal of professionalism by an entire "team" of employees, each specialists in their own area, and each committed to the overall success of the firm.

"Salaried" does not necessarily mean that the agent's earnings are capped or that there is no more incentive for increased production. There need to be both immediate and long-term benefits associated with top performance. Immediately, there is nothing in the salaried structure that prevents the payment of additional commissions or bonuses for specific performance goals. The flat salary (and benefits) could cover a certain expected base performance level. This could be calculated on a quarterly, semiannual or annual basis with additional commission kicking in after a certain base has been achieved.

Additionally, bonuses based on the company's overall performance—its ability to turn top-line revenues into bottom-line profits—are also beneficial and an important part of the compensation package. In such instances, however, the individual employees must feel that they are able to contribute to the profitability of the company and that they have some voice in decisions which may impact short or long-term profitability.

Long-term incentives involve building a future with the company—and staying there until retirement. Profit sharing and retirement plans play a strong role in this area. In fact, when a company gains a reputation as a good place to work, a leader in the business community, a name that brings value to the employee's association, then the mere fact of being employed by such a company and having the opportunity to grow with such a company becomes a long-term benefit in itself.

Growth opportunities must also be provided at every step of the way.

The new recruit just starting out in a clerical position (unlicensed assistant) should be able to see a career path in the company that will lead to additional responsibilities, increased income potential and long-term financial and personal benefits that will drive the recruit to learn, to take additional courses and to move into positions of greater responsibility. If the recruit has sales potential, then moving into a licensed assistant capacity would mark a major milestone in his/her development and growth with the company.

He or she would probably begin by performing some of the tasks related to listing and marketing the home and would also become involved in selecting and showing homes to interested buyers. Then, graduating to the rank of sales associate and working under the guidance of a skilled mentor—one of the company's successful agents—he or she would become involved in negotiating agreements between buyers and sellers, counseling buyers on financing options, and many of the other "professional" roles requiring a great deal of knowledge and experience.

There also need to be opportunities for those whose skills and personal interests point them more in the direction of management: either sales management, with the responsibility of working with a team of sales agents; or office management, taking on the day-to-day responsibilities of managing the physical plant, handling human resources, payroll, accounting, settlement services, etc. (Note: sales managers and general office managers are most often talents that do not—and should not be forced to—reside in one individual.)

Some of the company's personnel may have talents and interests of an entrepreneurial sort. There should be room in the company's overall plan to allow for such talents to be nurtured and developed within the company rather than losing such talents when such persons decide to leave the company and start out on their own. (In that case, the talent that you have developed can become your strongest competition.)

In order for this to happen, the company needs a growth plan that will allow those individuals who have demonstrated their abilities, loyalties and ambition to move into an ownership position with the company. This is generally accomplished either through an employee stock purchase program or through some form of profit-sharing arrangement. These are obvious tried-and-true formats, but do not necessarily challenge the real entrepreneurial spirit.

But consider an expansion program that would specifically target agents who have reached a certain pinnacle of performance and who are chafing at the bit to get into business for themselves. The company's expansion plan would identify business opportunities in the metropolitan area, targeting locations where new offices should be opened. As the timing is right, the company would build out those offices under the management of one of their best brokers who would eventually earn a significant ownership interest in that office.

What would eventually evolve would be a hub-and-spoke configuration, in which the main office would provide a host of support services to the spoke offices—central accounting, payroll, benefits management, human resources, marketing/advertising, training, computer services, printing, etc. The hub would also develop alliances with other service providers—mortgage, title, property management services, etc.—all the things that can most efficiently be done with larger volumes of business.

This would create a variety of new responsibilities for development of other business units within the company—and additional employment and advancement opportunities in all areas of the business.

The concept is not as strange as it may sound, and there is a significant example to be studied right in the real estate industry itself:

A 1988 *Inc. Magazine* article, "The Real Art of the Deal," by Nelson W. Aldrich, describes how Dallas real estate entrepreneur Trammell Crow built his multi-billion dollar empire on the principal of creating wealth—for himself and for others—through a unique partnering program:

"Wherever there were good real estate deals to be made, and good people to make them with, Trammell Crow would pick up partners. He moved through the cities of the land, trailing behind him one young partner after another, each of them inspired with the deal-maker's spirit, each of them very smart and very competitive, and most of them to become, thanks to him, very rich."

The article cites the example of Tom Shutt, Crow's first in-house leasing agent and the first in a long line of partners that Crow established:

"I'd been working for him for about eighteen months," Shutt says, "and one day Trammell comes up to me and says, 'We're going to be partners.' No papers, nothing to sign. I didn't know what he meant. I don't think he did. I just knew it was better than being an employee."

The fifty-fifty partnership initially involved a thirty thousand square-foot building in an industrial park in southwest Dallas, with Crow supplying the credit and know-how and Shutt supplying the sweat and the time. Crow would locate the land, outline the deal, then turn everything over to Shutt, who would oversee the purchase and building of the facility and the subsequent space leasing.

A few years later, Shutt was operating as a fifty-fifty partner developing Trammell Crow's operations in St. Louis, still working on Crow's credit and reputation, but otherwise totally independent.

Over the next twenty-five years, Crow used the same partnership strategy to bring more than two hundred additional partners on board. By 1978, fifteen of Trammell Crow's operating partners had become millionaires, several of them worth more than $10 million.

One requirement that Trammell required of his would-be partners was that they all had to work their way up through the ranks ("career pathing"), from leasing agents to project partners, then divisional partners, regional partners and finally national partners. A profit sharing program was developed for partners at every level.

By 1998, Trammell Crow had been ranked as

one of the nation's largest managers of commercial real estate for the ninth consecutive year, with 150 offices in the United States and Canada, and nearly five hundred million square feet of managed and/or leased space throughout the nation.

A PROFIT SHARING/RECRUITING MODEL

A student of the Trammell Crow model, Gary Keller, founding partner of Keller Williams Real Estate and the Keller Williams franchise network, built his franchise system around a "partnering" concept: The agents would be partners with the broker through a unique profit-sharing plan that would transcend the boundaries of each locally-owned and operated Keller Williams office.

Keller's plan is based upon the real estate company's need to recruit and retain good agents. Any Keller Williams agent who recruits another agent into the system will earn a share of the profit generated by that agent as long as the recruited agent remains in the system.

The recruited agent can go to work in a Keller Williams office two thousand miles from the office in which the recruiting agent works. The recruiting agent can move to another office—or can exit the business entirely—and the profit-sharing checks continue to arrive in his or her mailbox, provided only that the recruiting agent stays with the company for at least three years and the recruited agents continue to contribute to profit.

In order to establish credibility and a spirit of partnership among the agents and between agents and broker/owner, one of the requirements of the Keller Williams system is that the company's books be open to all agents. A central accounting system provides an analysis of each office's operations, and profit-sharing checks are issued directly from that central office. Agent councils are established within each office, each region and nationally, and all major decisions are made through those councils.

FORGET THE TOP, WATCH THE BOTTOM: IT'S WHAT GOES TO THE BANK THAT COUNTS

In order for any compensation structure to make sense, both the company and the agent have to adopt a bottom-line focus—what goes to the bank—rather than the traditional emphasis on the top line, or "production." How much is the ten million dollar producer taking to the bank, after paying all of the marketing and personal promotional expenses, and hiring and managing the personal assistants required to manage that much business?

From the company's perspective, how much profit is being realized from the production of top agents who are at astronomical commission splits?

Agents and managers also have to take a close look at the amount of hours that are being worked in order to achieve these production goals and compare that to the number of hours that would be required if the agent were working in a "team" configuration, where much of the work involved in the transaction is done by others, and the agent is involved only in those processes where the skills and experience of a seasoned agent are required. In this configuration, the salaried agent would handle a greater number of transactions, but would not work a greater number of hours.

And as the "team" concept is fine tuned, the cost of handling each transaction would gradually be reduced, with each part of the process being handled in a highly efficient manner by the team members specifically trained and assigned to those tasks. Top-line production, both for the company and for the individual agent, would then increase. Companies would then either have to find new ways to generate more business and/or reduce staffing to match the more streamlined systems.

THE PROFESSIONAL EMPLOYER ORGANIZATION

Movement into an employee relationship for real estate agents will be facilitated by the advancement of a relatively new business called the "Professional Employer Organization." Although an outgrowth of the temporary employee service industry, the PEO is specifically designed to provide total human resources management at all levels of employment—from the company's CEO all the way down to the mail room clerk—on an outsourced basis.

The concept is quite simple: The employees of the client company become employees of the PEO and are "leased back" to the client. From the perspective of the real estate broker-owner or manager this may sound a bit scary, as sales people are the real estate company's most valuable assets. However, PEO agreements are quite comprehensive and provide rather extensive protection of both the privacy rights of the individual employees and the client's proprietary rights to the employees so leased.

The purpose of the arrangement is to create a very large "pool" of employees for whom personnel and payroll services will be rendered. Because of the pooling, there is an economy of scale that not only makes handling all the paperwork more efficient, but also provides significant bargaining power when negotiating with suppliers of benefits programs (health insurance, retirement, etc.).

Whereas an individual real estate company may have twenty, two hundred, or two thousand employees, the PEO manages personnel services for dozens or even hundreds of companies, building an employee base of tens of thousands.

Payroll, federal, state and local taxes as well as all federal, state and local compliance issues are handled by the PEO.

There are a number of generic PEOs operating in most major marketplaces nationwide at this time, most of which are local or regional in scope. However, there is not yet in place a PEO specifically designed to service the real estate industry. Some real estate companies are already experimenting with PEOs for their management and administrative personnel (including licensed and unlicensed personal assistants). However the service could easily be adapted to include sales personnel as well. Only a minimum base salary is required in order to qualify for inclusion in a PEO program, and commissions, bonuses, draws or other alternatives to straight salary are all compatible and can be administered by the PEO.

Expect to see the major franchise organizations

experimenting with their own proprietary PEOs in the very near future. Beyond the direct revenue stream that would be produced by a PEO organization, such a proprietary system would help build franchise loyalty and create an additional dependence of the franchisee on the franchiser for maintenance of this service.

This may also be an area that Realtor associations or Multiple Listing Services may opt to enter. Or a totally separate entity may roll out a PEO service geared to the real estate industry.

The PEO customizes employee manuals for each client company, blending the company's own culture and business philosophy with standard text and documentation needed to provide whatever disclaimers, explanations, waivers and other language to provide legal protections for the client.

A PEO program specifically designed for the real estate brokerage industry would outline job descriptions for each position within the company, spelling out clearly the relationship between the company and its agents, detailing career advancement expectations, and providing legally binding employment agreements binding the employee to the employer and detailing both the reasons and specific processes for termination of the relationship. The employee manual would also spell out the specific benefits provided by the company. Each employee would receive a personalized copy detailing the specific benefits provided at that employee's level within the company.

While a large number of real estate companies may utilize the services of the same PEO, each company would have complete freedom in selecting the kinds of benefits programs it wishes to provide and the levels of company participation in such programs.

Since the PEO becomes an integral part of the relationship building process with all of the firm's personnel, its continued performance is extremely critical. Failure to meet payroll, poor service in benefits management or, worse yet, the loss of benefits programs through mismanagement—could prove disastrous to employee relations! For this reason, broker/owners interested in pursuing the possibilities that such services may offer should be advised to research these companies carefully, discuss their performance with existing clients (and past clients, if any), and do as much comparison shopping as possible.

NEW STRUCTURES

Agent compensation and benefits will no doubt be one of the major issues confronting the brokerage company of the future.

Most pundits predict that the "Internet Empowered Customer" will be doing more of the work involved in the home purchase, home selling process, and that other service vendors will continue to whittle away at what has traditionally been the role of the Realtor. This will inevitably mean that the price the consumer is willing to pay for the Realtor's involvement in the transaction will likely be reduced proportionately. All of this will require a rethinking of service delivery systems, staffing requirements and compensation structures.

If the real estate industry moves toward "unbundled" service delivery systems, where customers select from a menu of services and pay only for those services rendered, the salaried mode, with specific job assignments for each employee, would become an even more efficient and effective compensation structure.

The same would hold true for companies that implement a "one-stop" concept, where employees become involved in a variety of services other than those traditionally associated with "listing" and "selling."

Viewed in isolation from all the other changes on the horizon, it would seem doubtful that there would be much impetus from either the sales agent side nor from the brokerage management viewpoint to make the shift to the employer/employee relationship. Neither brokers nor agents will be excited about the prospects of these changes.

The impetus for change will no doubt be driven more by forces external to the brokerage industry itself—including shareholder demand for profitability and consumer demand for pricing and service—than by any movement from within.

Chapter 8:

The Future of Licensing and Education

Changes in the industry will be reflected by changes in both licensing requirements and educational programs and services.

The growth of e-commerce will have a decided impact on licensing and education, as new modes of delivery of real estate services will no doubt inspire new licensing requirements and impact the delivery of educational programs and testing services, as well as designation and certification programs.

The Association of Real Estate Licensing Law Officials (ARELLO) is currently in the process of developing standards of practice for cyberspace real estate operations. (ARELLO is not itself a regulatory authority, but is an association of state licensing law officers whose purpose is to attempt to standardize practices and procedures throughout the nation. Its recommendations often become the basis for action by state legislators and regulatory authorities.)

One of the issues ARELLO is grappling with is whether companies that offer Internet real estate services should be required to be licensed as real estate brokerage firms, since they are already involved in providing detailed information on listings and many of the other services traditionally associated with the brokerage firm. As they move closer to actual online transactional services, those sites may become the target for additional licensing requirements.

Another question involves the identification of real estate licensees on websites and e-mail correspondence. ARELLO will probably recommend that the inclusion of license numbers be mandatory in such communications to allow consumers to properly identify licensees with whom they become involved in e-commerce transactions.

And this is just the tip of the iceberg. It is almost a sure bet that licensing authorities will take every opportunity to regulate and extract additional licensing fees as e-commerce comes of age in the real estate industry.

Emerging trends in the industry and in the world of e-commerce may also advance the case for "single licensing"—where all real estate licensees would be required to have the equivalent of a broker's license and have the full responsibilities normally associated with the broker's license. The '90s saw the rapid advance of "company within the company" operations, where top producing agents hire a cadre of "personal assistants." This practice, coupled with the growing number of 100-percent commission operators, has created a degree of independence among sales agents previously unknown in this industry. Add to this the fact that in many companies the concept of a "managing broker" is already more fiction than fact, as sales agents literally "own" their customers and in many instances managing brokers have little knowledge of what is happening between agent and customer until a contract comes across their desk. Licensing authorities will likely move toward placing more responsibility directly on these independent licensees.

As "unbundling" occurs, and a variety of services once bundled together as part of the "listing" agreement become available on a menu selection basis, the direct services of the real estate salesperson will be limited to those areas requiring his or her specific training and expertise (counseling, pricing, negotiating, for example), and many of the functions previously associated with the licensee will be performed by clerical and administrative personnel within the company. This will open up new areas for licensing authorities to explore, and a variety of other categories of licenses may evolve.

As companies become more involved in the "one-stop-shopping" concept, additional services—mortgage, title, insurance, appraisals, home inspections, etc.—will all come under the umbrella of the real estate brokerage firm. And since the brokerage firm operates under state licensing authority and is therefore seen by the public as "authorized" to do business and, supposedly "regulated" in some fashion, the manner in which ancillary businesses are conducted within the licensed firm may also come under the scrutiny of licensing authorities.

The flip side of one-stop shopping will involve

companies not previously associated with real estate who are now adding real estate to their laundry list of services. This will be particularly evident in the world of e-commerce, where companies like HomeSpace Inc., which bills itself as "the nation's full service homeowner's portal" will be offering real estate services as part of its full-service menu. (HomeSpace, Inc. originally known as "AmeriNet," entered the business as a mortgage clearinghouse to provide discounted services to affinity groups.) HomeSpace offers mortgages from more than sixty national and regional lenders, as well as discounts on homeowner services, including home inspections, warranties, home security systems, insurance, long-distance telephone services, home improvement services and interstate moving. The company advertises that it "offers the largest national network of real estate brokers providing cash savings to home buyers and sellers."

The licensing issues that will be raised here will revolve around whether these companies themselves are real estate brokerage operations and what their relationship will be to individual licensees with whom they contract for real estate services. Previous rules and regulations with regard to "referral" operations may apply. Or, as these online companies become more directly involved in all aspects of the transaction, they may be seen more as the provider of the service through contracted licensees than as simply the referring source.

These issues—and many more which have not yet even come to light—will have a dramatic impact on the entire world of real estate licensing and regulation.

EDUCATION

The world of real estate education will also be dramatically changed during the coming decades. A heightened dependence upon technology, both in drawing the consumer into the real estate company and for the ultimate delivery of services to the consumer, will result in the need for additional specialized training in technology and technology-related issues for a variety of positions within the typical real estate company.

CONTENT

A great deal of education required for the staffing and operation of the real estate company of tomorrow will involve subjects not directly related to the purchase and sales of real estate. Business subjects, financial and accounting, management and human resource topics, computer-related courses and information retrieval, interpretation and management—anything relating to the myriad of skill sets that will be part of the multi-faceted world of the real estate brokerage company of the future.

There is a tremendous lack of focus on the "business" issues involved in establishing and growing one's real estate career. As more and more entrants to the industry will be coming in with college degrees, existing licensees need to be given the opportunity to educate themselves in such a fashion that they will be competitively positioned *vis-a-vis* these new entries.

Personal business management, financial management, time management—all should be part of the repertoire of courses that make up the real estate curriculum. Career real estate professionals should be taught how to build their clientele base in such a fashion that it becomes their "book of business"—a commodity that has market value should they become incapacitated, or otherwise unable to continue in the business, or at such time that they opt to retire. They should be taught financial planning early in their professional careers. This is a skill set that they can use to help keep their own careers on track as well as in counseling buyers, sellers and investors.

Some top producing agents will no doubt want to move out on their own, in partnership with a few of their peers, to create a limited liability corporation or partnership (LLC or LLP) much as those common to the legal or medical profession. They will need education as to how to do structure such an enterprise as well as in the day-to-day operation of that business.

And since within the real estate company of the future—be it the twenty-office megabrokerage firm or the small three-partner ten-employee company—a number of business and professional skill sets unrelated to real estate will be needed to ensure both a high level of customer service and ongoing profitability for those involved in the business.

DELIVERY

The manner in which education is delivered will also be drastically changed, as distance learning rapidly replaces the on-site classroom experience.

And the players in the real estate education field will also change as a result. The small, independent real estate school will be challenged by the need to develop additional curricula and distance learning applications. This challenge will be heightened by the fact that large national players are gearing up to dominate this field.

While the local entrepreneurial real estate school's competition in the past was primarily the educational programs offered by the major franchises, the field of competition will now include large national educational providers.

Distance learning, whether delivered by CD-ROM, satellite TV or the Internet, will dominate the world of real estate education in the future. And this can turn out to be either a boon or a disaster for the locally-based proprietary real estate school.

On the "boon" side, bringing people into a class-room facility and putting them in front of an instructor has become a rather expensive way in which to conduct educational programs. From the school's point of view, maintaining classroom facilities and keeping good trainers on the payroll is a major cost factor.

Bringing the student into the classroom, however, is much the same as bringing the shopper into the aisles of the department store or mass merchandising warehouse. Once in face-to-face contact with the customer, additional sales opportunities present themselves. For example, the student who enrolls in a real estate course will probably also purchase books and other "tools of the trade" while coming into the educational (and sales) facility on a regular basis while taking the course. Further, students who come on site for one course may be lured into yet another during the course of the training period.

Coming to the school for a required CE course

may trigger enrollment in a course leading to a designation program or a course related to some specific specialty (e.g. consumer financial counseling).

A combination of on-site delivery and home study will probably win the day. The on-site delivery, occurring perhaps at the beginning and/or end of the course, will comprise a very small percentage of the learning hours, utilizing few classroom and instructor hours. The home study will make up the bulk of the learning experience, with the opportunity for distance interaction with instructor at various points along the way. The classroom segment(s), where students can interact with fellow students and instructor, ask questions and generally feel a part of the ongoing process, would be essential both for assurance that the material was assimilated by the students and to give instructors and course developers a better idea of what else might be needed, how students react to the delivery of the course material, etc.

As opportunities emerge to provide ongoing education in a variety of new areas of specialization, and as competitive pressures develop in the form of Internet-based learning delivered by a variety of national providers, proprietary real estate schools are going to have to sharpen their edge and find venture partners for the development of both course material and distribution systems. New opportunities for expansion may come through partnering with various distance learning providers who may want the combination of electronic delivery of course content and the facilitated learning experience available through local schools that provide both the classrooms and the instructors.

The real estate schools located in highly populated urban centers fill their classrooms predominantly with students from the metro area who are within reasonable driving distance from the school. Many local schools also put their show on the road by renting meeting facilities in a number of cities around the state and then promoting their schedule of classes statewide. This allows them to further capitalize on the efforts and expense required to develop courses, curriculum and faculty, and exposes them to a much wider buying audience.

If the local school can develop programs that can be delivered in a distance-learning format, then it can expand its market base without ever expanding its physical facility or investing in facility rentals. Further, those local students who attend classes at the school's facility may decide to purchase additional training modules that they can take home and complete via distance learning.

While distance learning may provide new income opportunities for the proprietary schools, the cost of creating and producing courses in a distance-learning format can be prohibitive for an individual real estate school.

The major national franchises will no doubt develop entire syllabi of courses for distance learning delivery, and, if done well and delivered efficiently to their franchisees, such offerings may cut into the available market for the local real estate school.

In addition to the national real estate franchises, other entities will no doubt discover that developing educational programs specifically geared to the real estate industry and delivering them via distance learning can be a major source of revenues.

One such company is Kaplan Schools, a division of the Washington Post Company. Kaplan had its start back in the '50s, when standardized testing for college admissions was just beginning. The company made its mark by becoming the nation's leading provider of test preparation courses, for both undergraduate and graduate degree programs, as well as for a variety of professional certification programs.

In 1998, Kaplan purchased Dearborn Financial Publishing, the nation's leading provider of real estate educational programs and materials. The company is currently rolling out a variety of Internet-based educational programs and will likely develop a variety of distance learning products to cover all aspects of the "one-stop" shopping real estate industry.

What role will major colleges and universities play?

Consider Columbia School of Law, the California-based "cyber-school" that began operations in 1998 and whose campus exists only in cyberspace. Columbia's law curriculum has been recognized by the State of California, and graduates of the cyber-university are qualified to sit for the state bar exam.

Nearly ninety percent of the universities and colleges in the United States already offer off-site courses. The University of Maine System Network reaches nine thousand students in over 100 satellite classrooms.

An increasing number of colleges and universities have already begun offering graduate and postgraduate degrees in real estate and real estate related subjects. The University of Denver's Franklin Business School of Real Estate and Construction Management has instituted a two-year Masters in Real Estate program which involves eight one-week sessions on campus, with the rest of the instruction delivered through independent study and online sessions. Accordingly, the proprietary real estate schools may well experience increasing direct competition from the world of academia.

This would seem to point the real estate education world in one of several possible directions:

1) The vast majority of training will be done by just a few national entities; including several of the national real estate franchise organizations and one or more companies such as Kaplan who are large enough and progressive enough to move quickly into this arena.

2) One or more coalitions of proprietary schools, such as the ICE (Inner Circle Educators) Group may move aggressively into the distance learning arena, developing courses that can be rolled out through their individual member schools. While course development would prove too costly (and would move too slowly) if left to the devices of an individual local proprietary school, producing for several dozen proprietary schools could prove time- and cost-effective.

3) The national training companies and/or colleges and universities will either form alliances with or acquire large local and regional proprietary schools. The national companies will supply course materials and distance learning programs and the local school will provide the classrooms, facilitators and student management.

All of this will move the industry much closer to standardization of training and educational requirements for real estate licensing and continuing education. While each state will no doubt maintain tight control over its licensing authority and will regulate the course requirements for both pre-licensing and continuing education required to maintain a license, the actual content of the courses required will become homogenized, particularly when very good course offerings on a host of real estate specific topics become available from national suppliers.

There would seem to be a message in all this for the Realtor associations that are actively involved in the educational process.

In the future, as the educational process becomes even more complex, and as large national companies continue to enter the arena, the state and local associations' roles in the educational process may be seriously challenged.

Establishing relationships with existing educational providers might prove to be a better course of action than attempting to continue to provide their own proprietary products. To the extent that local and state organizations have already established themselves as credible players in the delivery of real estate education, they could bring unique value to a partnership with course developers. If they see themselves as competitors with the proprietary schools, and especially with the large national educational entities, they will surely see the industry move around them to establish its hold on their local markets.

Chapter 9:

The Future of Franchise Organizations

Going into the twenty-first century, the "Big Six" major franchise brands are Century-21, Coldwell Banker and ERA, all under Cendant ownership; Prudential, RE/MAX and Better Homes & Gardens (now owned by GMAC and in the process of phasing out the Better Homes & Gardens name and replacing it with the GMAC Real Estate image.)

Not to be ignored, however, are Realty Executives, and Keller Williams. Realty Executives is a national franchise with a stronger presence and market share in certain regional markets (such as Phoenix and the Northwestern suburbs of Chicago) than it enjoys nationally. The Realty Executives 100 percent concept has often been mistakenly dubbed a "knock off" of the RE/MAX program. As a matter of fact, Realty Executives was utilizing the concept long before RE/MAX came into existence. Before moving to Colorado, RE/MAX founder Dave Liniger actually worked as a sales associate in a Realty Executives office.

Keller Williams also deserves notice as a rising star in the franchise world. This organization is rooted in traditional real estate practice, but with a strong emphasis on "partnering" between the broker/owner and the agents. Keller Williams has adopted a unique profit-sharing program that rewards agents for bringing other agents into the system. The company's philosophy is built on a team approach to building profit, and from the individual local office through each region and on up to its national operations, decisions are made largely on input from agent "councils."

RE/MAX would seem to be a franchise that will continue to stand alone for a number of reasons.

Built largely on the charisma of its founder, Dave Liniger, RE/MAX has attracted a unique breed of highly independent agents who have seized upon the opportunity to literally run their own businesses while enjoying the benefits of a strong national image, the opportunity to associate with others of like ilk through regional, national and international programs and events.

But the glue that holds this group together, its fiercely independent entrepreneurial spirit, could well be the franchise's undoing, depending upon the ability of the franchise's leadership and its vision of the future. The highly successful independent agents of the future may opt to transplant their "company within the company" into partnerships with like-minded successful entrepreneurs, particularly if a national network or franchise were formed to help them do so.

Some also question whether the concept would continue to flourish without the personal magnetic leadership of its founders. However, the company has built a strong leadership team, many of whom have been with the organization since its earliest days, and who are deeply imbued with its founder's business philosophy, and recognized throughout the franchise system as being "in the trenches" and not some distant corporate executives.

One might also question the future profitability of the international franchise company, particularly since it has reached a state of maturity, where new franchise sales become a dwindling source of revenues.

Certainly all of these issues—the personal involvement of its founders, the independence of its agent base and the state of maturity that the franchise has achieved—raise questions regarding the attractiveness of the RE/MAX franchise as an acquisition target.

INTO A WHOLE NEW WORLD

One thing is certain, the world of franchising will never be the same—the same, that is, that it was in its earlier days. The entry of the big Wall Street and financial giants into the world of franchising has already had a dramatic impact on its future direction.

At first, the franchise was considered a haven for smaller companies, banding together, as it were, to create some of the clout that larger brokerage firms enjoyed. The role of the franchise was primarily to provide a name awareness that could make smaller local players seem "larger than life" in their marketplaces.

Particularly with the advent of the giants from the outside—Cendant and GMAC—that picture has

changed considerably. An increasing number of very
large firms are now sporting franchise colors, and franchised operations account for a very large percentage
of the residential real estate business.

Considering that the three brands owned by
Cendant—Century 21, Coldwell Banker and ERA—
encompass more than two hundred thousand licensees, it seems logical to predict that the franchise world
will have a tremendous role in shaping the future of
the industry. Couple this with the fact that the major
franchise owners—Cendant, GMAC, Prudential—either have their own business units that are involved
in a host of real estate related services, not the least
among them being mortgage companies), or have established strong business relationships with real estate related services. As such, they are poised to be
leaders in the "one stop shopping" trend.

Consider also that the new world of franchising
will be influenced more by the "Wall Street" mentality—building shareholder value, developing "brand"
names—than previous iterations of the franchises
which retained a more traditional "real estate" mentality. Unfortunately, the "real estate" mindset is focused on top-line productivity rather than bottom-line
profitability and has not been closely attuned to major trends affecting the larger world of commerce.

This will mean that some of the "sacred cows" of
the industry, the practices heretofore considered "giv-
ens," the attitudes and business philosophies that
dominated the world of real estate in the past, will
largely disappear in the shift toward a stronger focus
on "shareholder value." The franchisers will likely lead
the charge into such practices as menu driven service

delivery, giving consumers a great many options as to the level of service they wish to purchase—and the price they want to pay; the abandonment of the independent contractor concept, where agents work on straight commission, in favor of an employee relationship, where agents have a base salary, company benefits and a variety of incentive bonus arrangements.

The traditional "listing" concept will likely be abandoned in favor of a "marketing agreement" which provides a variety of menu-driven services for the seller, along with fee-based professional property valuation, consultation, negotiation and closing services.

The combination of advances in communications, including computerless access to Internet through cable and satellite services; the transition from the private ownership of information by the various MLS systems to completely open access to this information (and much more) by the general public on the Internet; and the aggressive battle for control of the gateway to the customer that is being waged by both the non-real-estate components to the transaction (mortgage, title companies) and the "Wall Street" ownership of the franchises ("affinity marketing" arrangements)—all this has to be taken into account when trying to get a fix on where the real estate industry will be ten to twenty years hence—and specifically what role the franchises will play in that transition.

MORE FRANCHISES OR FEWER?

Will there be more franchises, or fewer? Conventional wisdom says that the number will probably remain about the same. However, the ownership of the various brand names may be further consolidated.

The latter half of the '90s saw the consolidation of three major franchise brands under a single corporate entity. However, all three brands have been maintained as separate entities, each having its own unique "flavor" and operated in a very independent fashion.

Over the years, there has been some speculation as to whether Cendant might acquire a fourth brand. But unless a fourth brand would bring something to the mix that is not already there, it would seem unlikely that there would be any benefit to such an acquisition. Some have even considered that an acquisition of RE/MAX would make some sense, both from the consumer marketing point of view and from the brokerage management side. The red, white and blue balloon has certainly established its presence in a number of major markets. From the point of view of agent recruiting, having a strong 100-percent option within the family of franchises might make some sense.

Unlike the other "Big Six" franchise organizations, RE/MAX is a closely held family corporation. The personal pride of ownership in the Liniger family and the close ties which Dave and Gail Liniger have maintained with their franchisees would make an acquisition much more difficult. Even were the owners amenable to an acquisition (which they have not been in the past), it is questionable whether an acquisition could be profitable. Beyond any analysis of the company's financials, there would be the question of continuity after the acquisition. Due diligence would have to not only determine the extent of the company's current profitability, but also the viability of the franchise under a different corporate umbrella. It would not be an easy call.

Going into the new millennium, GMAC is making its first moves into ownership of real estate companies and wrestling with the name and identity changeover for its newly-acquired BH&G franchise. The company will likely follow the lead of the Cendant/ NRT model, achieving critical mass in regional markets by acquiring market leaders and placing them into the GMAC "brand." No doubt the company will also encourage—and even participate in—mergers and acquisitions among its existing franchisees to further bolster the brand name's image by converting a number of smaller, less visible firms into single larger entities, then establishing these newly merged entities as "hubs" around which the region can be built out.

There has been some speculation that GMAC will also follow the Cendant pattern in acquiring one or more other franchise brands. But it seems unlikely that this will happen. One of the primary objectives of the GMAC acquisition seems to have been to enhance the position of GMAC Mortgage in the marketplace. The company is already beginning to phase out the familiar and revered Better Homes & Gardens name and image in favor of its own GMAC Real Estate brand name.

If another national entity is in GMAC's acquisition sights, it would be for the purposes of maximizing market share and brand name recognition for its primary GMAC Real Estate Brand rather than to be operated as a competing brand name as in the Cendant/ NRT model.

One might question whether a company such as MidAmerican Energy and its newly established residential real estate network might be an acquisition target for either Cendant or GMAC.

MidAmerican is a midwestern utilities company seeking to solidify its lock on the homeowner as a purchaser of deregulated gas and electric power by establishing strong ties through local real estate operations. There would seem to be no direct conflict between MidAmerican's goals and those of either GMAC or Cendant, since the latter have not made any forays into the electric or natural gas utilities marketplace. Acquisition of these MidAmerican companies by NRT or GMAC could actually move MidAmerican's agenda more swiftly, assuming the deal carried with it opportunities to cross-market across all affiliated brands.

If MidAmerican has its sights set on further geographic expansion of its core utility business, then the immediate geographic coverage that either Cendant or GMAC could offer would also make sense.

And even if MidAmerican intends to make real estate a core business, operating real estate companies in just ten or eleven states in competition with the major national players would not seem to make a whole lot of sense. The company will either enter a national expansion mode, merge its real estate operations with one of the national giants, or acquire one of the other major brands.

Further complicating the picture, shortly after the company's real estate division, HomeServices.Com, completed an initial public offering in the fall of 1999, an investor group headed by Warren Buffett's Berkshire Hathaway announced that it had reached a definitive agreement to acquire MidAmerican.

NEW FRANCHISE ENTITIES

Beyond speculation on the direction that existing franchise operations will be taking, any discussion of the future of franchising should also address the possibility of the advent of entirely new franchise concepts.

New types of franchises may evolve for a number of reasons and focus around a variety of opportunities:

First, with the growing independence of the individual agent and the likelihood of a "single license" concept, where every agent will be required to operate under the equivalent of today's broker's license, the total number of agents will likely decrease, as top agents command a larger volume of business and develop their own "company within the company." In this scenario, the emergence of a franchise designed to provide specific services for the individual agent is a distinct possibility. Such a franchise could provide assistance in establishing limited liability partnerships or corporations in which a number of top producing agents would form their own company. The franchise would provide all the legal agreements, business plans, computer programming, etc. to establish and run the business. Such a franchise could also provide a turnkey human resources department for its franchisees, in the form of a PEO (Professional Employer Organization), providing a full range of payroll and tax accounting services, employee benefits, commission advance programs and a variety of other services to allow the individual agent-partners to maximize their time handling the professional contacts with customers rather than wasting time trying to run the business.

Another area which may spawn new franchise opportunities would be Internet services. Again, focusing on the individual agent, and considering the possibility of more and more agents operating under their own brokers licenses, a "cyberspace" real estate company could be established which would provide qualified leads to agent-franchisees who would supply the "high touch" element in the otherwise electronic transaction.

The consumer demand for "one stop shopping" capabilities could also drive the formation of another type of franchise. As the traditional franchises refine these operations for their existing franchisees, the vast number of smaller companies working without the benefits of a franchise will find it difficult to create similar programs in order to compete. However, a franchise system could be developed to provide turnkey one-stop shopping connections for the small independent company. Appealing to those who are reluctant to share a percentage of their real estate commissions with a franchiser, this new franchise entity would derive its revenues from advertising and "finders fees" paid by a host of related industries wanting to get in front of the home buying customer.

In light of the myriad of changes that will be influencing the future development of the real estate industry, it is logical that enterprising minds will find a similar array of opportunities for developing programs and services that can be provided to real estate practitioners on a franchise or "licensing" basis.

THE ROLE OF THE FRANCHISE SYSTEM

Franchise systems will play new roles in the development of the real estate industry of the future.

Building consumer awareness for their franchise brands will remain a primary focus. Brand loyalty will be built not only by maintaining a strong national advertising presence, but also by constructing a "total consumer experience" built around the delivery of a multitude of homeowner services by franchisees.

This will require some combination of strong affinity marketing relationships and/or a variety of company-owned service providers.

Another service of the franchise will be to provide an "exit strategy" for their franchisees by helping them build their businesses solidly; assisting them with mergers and acquisitions to further strengthen their businesses; and the addition of complementary business units—the traditional mortgage, title and insurance, as well as a broad array of "concierge" services— to broaden the base upon which profits are generated and to increase the firm's market value.

Part of this process may also involve the establishment of publicly traded entities which could acquire successful franchisee operations, providing both a management position and equity ownership for franchisees who wish to convert their privately held businesses into shares of publicly traded stock to provide both an "exit plan" and the added protection of a broad geographic business base, rather than one based on a potentially volatile local economy.

Another role of the franchise will be to provide assistance in the area of technology. In some instances, the national franchise will be the technology supplier, particularly in providing "back office" computerization and communications systems among members and between members and the franchiser's headquarters. In other instances, the franchise will outsource technology development, creating liaisons with existing hardware and software vendors for both the development of proprietary programs for use by franchisees and for the bulk pricing that only a large national entity could command.

As information moves away from its current shackles to the computer terminal and becomes available through cable modems and TV set-top boxes, the franchise will be uniquely positioned to provide the central server technology and support that will keep franchisees on the leading edge of this new technology. This translates into keeping the franchisee in closer touch with the Internet Empowered Consumer.

The franchise will also play a dominant role in teaching its franchisees to utilize technology efficiently, not only in developing leads and servicing clients and customers, but also in managing all brokerage operations. Central server technology will allow paperless monitoring of franchisee operations, instantaneous reporting between franchisee and franchise headquarters, and professional analysis and fine-tuning of the franchisees' business operations to maximize profitability for both the franchiser and franchisee.

All these functions will not only provide a valuable service for the franchisee, but will also help lock the franchisee into the franchise relationship, making the franchiser an essential "business partner."

Chapter 10:

The Future of Organized Real Estate

Any discussion of the future of "organized" real estate should be prefaced by a recognition of the fact that the National Association of Realtors, as well as the state and local Boards and Associations, have been a very strong force in shaping the business of real estate during nearly all of the twentieth century.

The Realtor associations have been the "glue" that has held the real estate industry together from its very insular mode of existence during the early decades of the century, where each member clung protectively to his own listing inventory, warily suspicious of any attempts to interfere with his client base, straight through into today's mode of operation where dependence upon the listing inventory of fellow Realtors has become a way of life.

During its first half-century, the National Association of Realtors was comprised of members who were generally from single-office firms, each with a handful of salespeople. Today, it represents an amazing mix of company size and configuration, some of them from companies with thousands of agents doing tens of billions of dollars in sales volume. (In 1998, the ten largest real estate companies in the nation had a total of more than 1,400 offices with sales volume of more than $150 billion.) Yet several hundred thousand members are still working within single-office firms, each with just a handful of agents.

According to *The 1999 National Association of Realtors Profile of Real Estate Firms*, eighty-two percent of residential brokerages have a single office, while only five percent have more than three offices. Fifty-one percent of residential brokers have a sales force of five agents or less, while five percent have a sales force larger than fifty. But thirty-eight percent of the association's membership is concentrated within that five percent. More than half the firms with ten or more agents are affiliated with a national franchise.

Maintaining viability while serving such a diverse mix has been a task that few organizations would have survived!

And while the survival of the Realtor organization may sometimes be thought of as just a way to satisfy the "association junkies" among us, having a strong organization to represent the interests of both the real estate professionals working in this industry and the home-owning public at large will become even more critical in the coming decades.

The structure of that organization may need some rethinking, however, to assure that it can deliver the services needed in the future.

Many conflicts have developed over recent years revolving around what the role of the National Association of Realtors—and the state and local associations as well—should really be, and whether or not the three-tiered structure (national, state, local) is still a viable model.

We need to realize that not only was the industry much more homogeneous in the first half of the twentieth century, but the methods of communication were extremely limited then, compared to those of the century just opening.

In the earlier days, long distance telephone communications were difficult and expensive. There were no fax machines, no conference calling, certainly no video conferencing.

Today's electronic communications, from inexpensive long distance conference calling, to the instantaneous (and free) two-way communications of e-mail, to Intranet systems allowing private communications channels for specific business operations—all this creates a communications platform that will radically alter the way in which national and worldwide organizations conduct their business.

A more serious concern has been raised regarding the involvement of the Realtor organizations in providing programs and services that are competitive with those being developed by some of the associations' largest members.

More than half of the membership of the Realtor organizations is now comprised of persons affiliated with either a large megabroker, a franchise or a nationally owned real estate entity. And more than half of the associations' dues revenues come from those sources.

The major franchises and nationally-owned companies are able to develop a myriad of programs and services that are not economically feasible for the smaller independent brokerage firm—such things as sales and management training programs; agent benefit programs (insurance, retirement); bulk purchasing agreements providing discounted prices on equipment, software, services, supplies; and affinity marketing programs.

The small broker who finds himself being outgunned by his franchised or nationally owned competitors, might look to the Realtor organization to provide tools that will help him compete—whether in the consumer marketplace or in recruiting and retaining good agents. Conversely, the large entities understandably balk when their dues dollars are used to create competitive marketing, advertising, educational or internal benefits programs (e.g. "Realtor Rewards") to help the little guy compete.

The prospect of serving either the interests of members in very large firms and franchises, or catering to the needs of members working in smaller companies seems to put the associations on the horns of a dilemma: serve the little guys and run the risk of losing the big ones; or cater to the big ones and lose the little ones—or perhaps lose all, as members in smaller firms find fewer reasons to belong and the bigger firms could eventually replicate most of the functions of the associations, rendering membership meaningless.

The solution may lie in carefully analyzing all of the activities the associations are involved in, then paring away any and all that can as readily be provided by others, focusing only on those that can best be accomplished by a strong association rather than by individual proprietary companies.

Should the Realtor associations continue to explore new "businesses" to get into—new products and services to add to their catalogue of member benefits? While this approach can provide new streams of revenue and add value to membership for those members in need of such products and services, it can also become a source of irritation for the growing number of members who work within large companies already offering similar services. They do not want to see their dues dollars spent developing and promoting programs and products that help smaller companies remain competitive with them.

Or should the goal of Realtor associations in the future become much more narrowly focused on those specific areas where they are uniquely able to fill a need for all members?

Lobbying, for example. Not even the largest national company or individual franchise—nor even a "consortium" of franchises—could have the lobbying clout of a national association that represents all real estate professionals.

Or consumer education. Campaigns to educate the consumer on a broad range of real estate-related issues will be most effective when coming from an industry-wide source rather than from an individual company.

The stories of the "evolutionary progress" that companies such as 3M and American Express experienced (see Chapter One) have great relevance for Realtor associations attempting to discover what their role in the future should be: Discover what the customer needs, then figure out how to deliver it.

For the Realtor associations, two "customers" need to be taken into consideration: the dues-paying customer, the Realtor member; and the Realtor's "customer," the home-buying and home-selling consumer. If one of the association's roles will be to keep its Realtor member a necessary and valuable part of the transaction, then positioning that member's services in the mind of the consumer is of paramount importance.

Direct education of the consumer in real estate and homeownership matters should become an increasingly more important role for the associations. Working in conjunction with local members, Realtor organizations should mount a consumer education program—not hyping how good Realtors are—but providing the interested homeowner with a sound basis to understand the investment value and opportunities that real estate offers as well as understanding the processes of buying, selling and financing.

As an organization we need to stop focusing on telling consumers how great we are, how educated we are, how dedicated we are, how hard we work for them, how well trained we are, and on, and on. Let the national franchises and local real estate companies advertise that. As a trade association let's focus on getting people to want our product!

Take the example of the "Got Milk?" campaign. Who in America has not seen the billboards, television and magazine ads with our heroes and superstars all sporting a milk mustache? Throughout that campaign, the American Dairy Council has focused not on how educated today's dairy farmers are in milk production techniques, nor how productive they are as an industry, and not even on how sanitary today's milk processing plants might be. Rather, they have launched an all-out campaign to get people to want to drink milk. "It's good! I drink it! It makes me strong...beautiful...appealing...successful" say the artists, entertainers and sports heroes. "Two glasses a day...one for each home run!" says Mark McGwire.

"Yes, but..." you say, "it's one thing to convince the public that they should buy a $3 bottle of milk. Quite another that they should buy a $180,000 home! After all, we buy things to drink everyday at the grocery store. We only buy a home once every seven years (or longer)."

True. But consider the automobile industry. The purchase of a luxury car is not exactly a small investment! Yet car ads on TV do not talk about how well educated your local automobile salesperson is. How he can help you make the right decision on a car purchase. How he can assist with all the paperwork associated with buying a car. Not at all. The focus is on speed, on chic, on luxury styling, on how good the car will make you feel, on how important it is to have the latest model. Good feeling! Prestige of ownership! The "Gotta have it" syndrome.

If someone told Detroit that the average consumer would only buy a new car every seven years, I don't think they'd roll over and re-structure their business model to meet that timetable. Rather, they'd go full bore into an advertising campaign to change it. Their bucks would be spent making people want to buy that new car.

So why does the average homeowner buy a home

only every seven to eight years?   Why are there so
many people renting their homes rather than making
the move into homeownership? Is there a way to create a market? To nudge the market a bit—or perhaps
even give it a big push?

We won't do that by telling the American public
how great we are. We need to tell them how great
owning a home is. And how easy it is. And we need to
make those who already own a home feel that moving
up is a good idea...that it is possible... that it will feel
good...and that it will be easy, fun and a rewarding
experience.

That means we have to make the process of trading in a home just about as simple as trading in a car.
And perhaps the Realtor associations need to do some
lobbying to eliminate some of the red tape and delays
associated with buying a home.

You can drive into the auto dealership and drive
back out in a new car in less than an hour—all details
handled. The insurance has been transferred, the title
and license applications have been handled, the financing is in place and, more than likely an extended warranty has been added. And if there are some bells and
whistles that you still want, the dealer will pick the
car up at your convenience, leaving a loaner for you to
drive, and return the car with pinstriping, phone or
sound system upgrade—or whatever, just to complete
the sale and create a satisfied customer. And they
know that if they make it a pleasant experience, you'll
probably be back to do it again.

One of NAR's roles should be to rally whatever
resources are necessary to simplify the home buying,
home financing process. The task would not be a

simple one, but as one of the nation's largest trade associations, NAR should be able to accomplish it—especially since the project has such a large consumer advocacy component. Other organizations, such as the Consumer Federation of America and AARP, often seen as the opponents of organized real estate, should be enlisted as allies in this cause.

Is there a way to reach the first-time buyer marketplace to get them to buy sooner? Do they know how easy it is? Do they realize how much money they would save paying their own mortgage instead of paying it for the landlord? Do they know how much fun it would be to own instead of rent? Do they know how much their equity will build up—and how soon? And can they do the deal quickly and without a lot of hassle?

Perhaps there's some advertising and education needed in that regard.

Do we have to wait for existing homeowners to decide it is time to make a move? Or should we be romancing the concept of moving to new digs the way the ADC romances drinking milk? Or the way an automobile dealer romances buying a new car?

KEEP THE REALTOR IN THE TRANSACTION

In addition to creating a demand for the product, there will be an increasing need to convince the home buying, home selling public to utilize the services of a Realtor in the transaction.

In the past, with Realtor control of the information via the MLS, it was really not much of a problem educating the American public to hire a Realtor rather than go the "For Sale By Owner" route. The only way to gain access to the MLS, whether as seller or buyer, was to go through a Realtor.

There was always the concern that the general public would not understand the difference between the generic term "licensee" and the proprietary tradename "Realtor." But that was a greater concern for the Realtor association than for its individual members, as it considered its value to its membership directly related to the value placed on its proprietary trade name "Realtor."

But all that has forever changed.

In the marketplace of the future, the challenge will be to convince the home-selling and home-buying public that it still makes sense to hire a professional, even though a growing number of alternatives are developing—both in cyberspace and with other companies not previously considered our competitors.

If there emerges an "Amazon.com" of the real estate world, or if companies such as Wal-Mart develop their own real estate marketing departments, both in-store and in cyberspace, then the challenge will be to guarantee that even in this delivery mode, there will be a role for the professional Realtor. To accomplish this, the public needs to be convinced that unless a Realtor is involved in the transaction, they may not be getting the best deal—even if the price seems right. And the ultimate role of the Realtor in such transactions will not only have to be beneficial to the consumer, but must also fit the profit picture for the mass merchandisers.

The alternative would be to mount a massive campaign against purchasing real estate through such mass market outlets. But I am not so sure how well even an organization as large as the National Association of Realtors would fare in that battle.

To keep new programs—be they Internet or the Wal-Mart variety—from eliminating the Realtor from the transaction, Realtor associations must do one of two things: Either

1) develop programs and services that really add value from the consumer's perspective and that cannot be replicated by these Internet or mass merchandising offerings; or

2) develop a role for the Realtor within the Internet and mass-merchandiser model.

Or perhaps we need to do both. The two are not mutually exclusive.

It should be a primary function of the Realtor associations to take the lead in analyzing those future scenarios and developing the programs that will keep the Realtor in the transaction. This does not mean attempting to create contrivances that will perpetuate existing industry practices. If the role of the Realtor needs to change in order to remain a value-added part of the transaction, then the Realtor associations need to invest the time, dollars and efforts required to reinvent that role and to teach their own membership how to adapt, as well as to teach the other service providers and the consumer public how to best utilize these adapted services of the Realtor.

CONVENTIONS

Is there a value to national conventions? Yes. But they should be focused on areas that only the association can provide and that can best be accomplished by bringing members together into the "convention" setting.

It never ceases to amaze me that Realtors will go to great expense attending a national convention and then spend a great deal of their time jumping from classroom to classroom to get CE credit hours when the same courses could have been taken back home— or even at home, through distance learning offerings.

The proprietary schools, the universities, the franchises and a myriad of private-label trainers and motivators deliver their educational product nation-wide all year long. One should not have to come to a convention to get that.

New course development, however, would be a reason to assemble in one classroom a divergent group of licensees from across the nation as well as repre-sentatives from every sector of the real estate educa-tion arena. This would provide a "beta test" opportu-nity for course developers to fine-tune existing mate-rial and to explore the development of entirely new educational opportunities. Suppliers of software pro-gramming could also be invited to participate in these sessions.

No longer a direct competitor in the education arena, NAR would also provide an arms-length course review and appraisal function. The actual delivery of educational programs—whether in classroom or via distance learning— would be the responsibility of pro-prietary schools, franchises and major national real estate entities.

NAR would act as the disinterested third-party, not as a competitor. Its interest in educational prod-uct would not be that of a supplier, but rather as the representative of hundreds of thousands of agents and millions of homeowner-consumers. Its purpose would be to make certain that the Realtor has all the educational resources available to remain on the cutting edge of the marketplace.

The national convention should also provide an opportunity for discussion of issues of importance to the industry and to homebuyers; a forum for feedback from the membership to the association; an interdisciplinary meeting ground where all industries relating to home ownership can meet and discuss their interrelated businesses; and a rallying point to bring all resources to bear on lobbying for more favorable legislation and creating strong incentives to move the market to even higher levels.

While input from grass-roots membership would remain an important part of the process, the role of the national association would also involve bringing new thinking into the process to lead membership into areas they would otherwise be unlikely to explore.

The supplier showcase at the national convention is invaluable, but more effort should be made to turn this into a learning experience for both real estate professionals and the variety of suppliers producing product for the industry: More on-site demonstrations of existing and coming tools and technology. More forums in which producers can interface with users to pinpoint new product opportunities. And much less of the junk that has been appearing at these events— from costume jewelry, to foot massagers, to T-shirts, to very tacky advertising and promotional gimmicks. (Want to have magic potions that will make you so alluring that customers will cling to you? You've seen them advertised in *Realtor Magazine* and can probably pick them up at the next Realtor convention!)

GOVERNANCE

When the direction of an organization depends upon bringing some eight hundred "directors" into concurrence, the process can be long and cumbersome, as anyone who has ever attended an NAR Directors meeting will attest. In the past, a major role of the national convention has been bringing the governing bodies of the association together to discuss issues and make policy. Advances in communications should allow this to become an ongoing process rather than one relegated to two or three face-to-face meetings each year.

In an age where change is occurring at lightning speed, and where some of the changes could impact the very foundations of the real estate industry as we know it today, the ability to shift gears, to move quickly and assertively could mean the difference between maintaining a leadership role or slipping into obsolescence.

Moving the association into the twenty-first century will require both a serious revamping of internal structures and a more creative utilization of emerging high speed communications processes—both for polling its membership on a regular basis and for keeping its membership informed about issues.

The association executive will play an even more critical role as the industry comes face to face with the realities of the marketplace of the future.

A principal role of leadership within Realtor associations needs to be that of bringing a new viewpoint—a new vision—to its membership. It is essential that true visionaries be hired for these positions and that their functioning not be hampered by the bureaucracy inherent in large organizations. Keeping the Realtor strategically positioned in the marketplace of the future will involve serious business decisions, some of which may actually run contrary to popular opinion among the membership.

While individual Realtor members must continue to be focused on the day-to-day operation of their businesses, association leadership needs to be empowered to lead its membership to new heights, rather than constrained to follow that membership down a time-worn treadmill to oblivion.

Realtor publications —newsletters, magazines, white papers—whether delivered electronically or in print format, whether coming from NAR, state or local association—need to expand their focus well beyond traditional "real estate" subjects. There is no argument that practitioners need to keep up with what is going on within their own industry. But, if they want to lead rather than follow, they need also to be watching very closely what is going on in a great many other areas, such as consumer trends and marketing, commerce and finance, even arts and entertainment.

Why did Wal-Mart buy a small Oklahoma bank? What is the significance of Microsoft's change in mission statement? What are IBM and Amway doing in the e-commerce world? What is going on in the world of electronic banking? Why would e-Bay launch fifty regional websites? How did Trammell Crow build its national empire? Why are some doctors going into the hospital business? Why are e-commerce marketers going on a warehouse-building boom? What is GM planning to do with its Web site? How do large accounting and consulting firms do their most effective recruiting?

Articles on these topics were found in business journals and newspapers published over just a three-month period. Most of them have no direct connection with real estate. But each of them provides a unique insight into some specific area of how other businesses are reinventing themselves in light of emerging trends and opportunities. An astute observer can find at least one specific connection with the residential brokerage industry in each of them. And taken together, they speak volumes about positioning a real estate company for the future.

One role of the association, therefore, could be to read and analyze such material on a day-to-day basis, digest it, make it the subject of surveys, of focus groups, of on-line and on-site discussion groups.

Convening of interdisciplinary groups for similar purposes and involving leaders from a variety of businesses would also be within the scope of Realtor associations—and a valuable strategic planning resource for both the associations and their members.

This is not to say that the associations are not already doing many such things. Rather, it is to say that the membership should not only demand such activities, but actively support them, participate in them, and profit from them.

MAINTAINING PERSPECTIVE

While we have only scratched the surface in looking at ways in which our Realtor organizations may be evolving in the future, one thing seems to stand out quite clearly: There has never been a greater need for organization and leadership within this industry.

However, it is extremely important to separate the role of protecting the future of the association itself from that of protecting the futures of its members.

Contrary to popular association management hype, the two are not inseparable. An association can survive for a long time without providing truly visionary leadership for its membership. Scientists would describe the process as one of "momentum." As a wise old president of the United States once noted, "a government agency is just about the closest thing to eternal life that we will ever experience on this earth." Once created and put in motion, some organizational structures seem to have a way of creating a life of their own.

Nor would the demise of the associations as we know them bring about the downfall of the real estate industry.

This should not be taken as a call for mutiny within the ranks. In fact, quite the contrary. Undermining the tremendously powerful machine that has already been built at just the moment in history when it will be most vitally needed would make no sense at all.

Rather, it is a reminder that the Realtor organizations can play a very instrumental role in giving their members a leadership position in the emerging new market opportunities of the twenty-first century.

But it is essential that members of the associations appreciate the real value of the machine their dues dollars have created—and insist that that machine be put to work solving the real problems that lie ahead, and not just memorializing the past.

Conclusion:

Making the Transition To the Future

Having explored a great many options and tried on a lot of "What Ifs," there comes a time when thinking has to turn into action; where dreaming has to turn into planning.

For the serious planner, "futuring" is an ongoing process not a static event.

A lifelong devotee of the real estate industry, Bud Smith (retired executive vice president of the National Association of Realtors), likes to use an analogy drawn from his experience as a bird hunter to describe a basic strategic planning rule:

"You have to know where to plant your feet," he says.

When you scare up the quail, there is no telling in what direction they will fly, he explains. Initially, they will probably all start to go straight up out of the brush, but for just a nanosecond. Then they may turn quickly in almost any direction, to left or right. In some instances they may fly directly toward the hunter. It is not just a matter of having the choke set appropriately, but also of having your feet planted in such a fashion that you can move and pivot quickly to have any kind of a shot. Not knowing where to plant one's feet can result in planting one's posterior instead!

As we said more than two hundred pages ago, there are no definitive answers. And there is no one, single path that can be determined at this point as THE path along which the industry will progress. There are just too many variables.

However, when we consider the various twists and turns that the business may take, it is possible to come up with some common threads that seem to tie it all together.

Reviewing all the possible transformations that may occur in our industry in the coming years—the possible changes that may occur—we need to be able to determine what degree of probability each may have before beginning any process of change to accommodate the future.

To help with our own assessment of future trends and directions, we engaged a number of "focus groups" made up of real estate broker/owners and executives from firms in a variety of markets across the continent. Then we boiled down the input from those sessions to determine what directions they felt seemed most probable.

Before sharing the findings of those focus groups, we should first add a disclaimer: The opinions shared at these sessions were those of industry practitioners, most of them broker/owners of fairly large-scale real estate companies. They are not the result of scientific study, nor of the findings of demographers, economists and business school professors, but rather of people who are in the trenches—and who may not always be able to see very far beyond the trenches.

We thought their insights would be invaluable for two reasons: First, their level of experience in the real world of real estate is unmatched in any academic setting. And, second, the way they see things should give some indication as to how many others in this industry are currently thinking. We have to know where we are coming from before we can figure out how to get where we want to go. And these folks know a lot about where we are coming from!

While we asked our focus group participants to bring their own thinking to the sessions, we also assigned some "required reading" to be done in advance. The assigned material included mostly non-real estate subjects, articles from general business magazines and professional journals.

They were asked to try to relate whatever they read to the real estate industry and to look for areas in which there were crossover applications.

It should also be noted that most of today's leaders in the real estate industry—at least those who are broker/owners and managers of brokerage firms—have grown up within the industry and tend to see things from a very practical, but narrowly focused viewpoint. Thinking "outside the box" has not been a hallmark of this industry. (Nor has it been for most proprietary businesses.)

As we analyzed the conclusions drawn by these

focus groups, we looked not only at what was said, but also for threads that might tie the various "futures" together. We specifically looked for ways in which opinions expressed about one specific aspect of the business future might help validate a much larger view when combined with opinions expressed about entirely different subjects.

As we report the results below, we will add our own editorial comments, indicating our interpretations of either what seemed to be behind the comments expressed or how certain conclusions seem to support— or contradict—others.

The views of the future developed within the focus groups are categorized as follows:

"Likely" describing events and directions that the majority of the group felt were imminent or most likely to occur.

"Far out" not in a chronological sense, but in their likelihood of happening. Not a highly probable, but certainly a possible direction for the future.

"Extreme" describing an outcome that is also not highly probable, but possible, and one that would have a drastic impact on the industry.

It was especially interesting to note that certain future trends that were categorized as "far out" seemed to dovetail precisely with futures that the groups considered "very likely" in other areas.

The value of this exercise lies in stimulating the thought processes. It is not reasonable that anyone would take any of the focus group conclusions as "The Gospel of the Future," but that each would use these conclusions as the starting point for formulating his or her own view of the future.

It is highly recommended that similar exercises be conducted periodically within a real estate company's management team, and perhaps at varying levels throughout the entire organization.

We are certainly not suggesting that strategic planning for the company become a matter of democratic vote. The final decisions as to what to implement and when must lie solely with those who are at risk for the results. However input in advance can provide new levels of insight. And having brought all parties to the table to brainstorm the future will help bring all parties to buy into whatever new directions are deemed appropriate.

All that being said, here are the conclusions that we were able to draw from our focus group sessions:

STRUCTURE OF THE BROKERAGE INDUSTRY OF THE FUTURE

Regarding the structure of the brokerage industry, the "most likely" future scenario is that there will be two distinctly different structures:

The first will be developed by what might be called the "Platform Owners"—companies such as utility companies, financial institutions and others whose core business has not been real estate and who see establishing a position in the real estate business as a platform or feeder for their primary business.

The other will be developed by those who consider real estate to be their core business—or one of their core businesses. These will be the large regional megabrokerage firms and the real estate franchise operations, including the Cendant family. (Although

Cendant is diversified into many industries other than real estate, its real estate division is considered one of its major business units, and real estate operations contribute substantially to the company's revenue stream and resulting shareholder value.)

This "most likely" scenario seems to be a continued progression of the ongoing trend toward consolidation under brand names that we have seen in the recent several years. It also allows for the continued existence of smaller firms, although their competitive position would seem to rely on discovering and developing niches in which they can provide a "total customer experience" different from that of the mega-companies.

These niche market players will be financially successful only if (and probably also because) the owners are directly engaged in the business.

The "way out" scenario is that seventy percent of the business will be consolidated within just a few—perhaps ten—entities. The massive capital investment and technology requirements will create a need for massive scale and hierarchical ownership.

An "extreme" future was also considered a remote possibility, one in which the real estate business would become totally disintermediated, and the brokerage industry as we know it disappears entirely.

OWNERSHIP OF THE CUSTOMER

Almost all were in agreement that at the present time, the customer is actually "owned" by the sales agents, not the company. Therefore, for all intents and purposes, the company itself is "owned" by the sales agents. This is evident in the fact that broker-owners and managers will do almost anything to keep a producing agent on board or to entice a producer from another firm to come on board. It is also evident in the commission-splitting structures in place in most firms today.

There was consensus that the "most likely" future is that "ownership" of the customer will shift away from being the rather exclusive domain of the sales agent to a position where the customer is jointly owned by the sales agent and the company. This would be more of a "partnering" mode.

The rationale behind this seems to be that with advances in communications and technology, customers will have direct access to a great deal of information previously obtainable only through a sales agent. Further, as companies become more sophisticated in their use of professional lead development techniques, initial access to customers as well as customer follow-up will move more into the domain of the company.

Throughout, however, the agent will remain an essential element in the transaction. Both the company and the agent will be directly involved with the customer at all stages, and will thus both "own" the customer together.

The "way out" future outlook says that as the real estate company becomes more of the "one stop shopping" source for a variety of homeowner related services, the company's direct involvement with the customer will strengthen even further. The brokerage firm will eventually regain complete control of the customer in order to assure that each customer has an "outstanding total experience" from start to finish.

The sales agents will still play a definitive role, but as service providers to customers developed and maintained by the company. Controlling the "total customer experience" will be necessary to justify the involvement of the brokerage industry in the transaction.

THE ROLE OF TECHNOLOGY IN THE FUTURE

There is almost universal agreement that penetration of technology into the brokerage industry at the present time is widely diverse. For a great many practitioners—brokers and agents alike—Internet applications are being adopted and implemented as gadgets or gimmicks, with little or no concept as to whether or not they are adding value to the consumer and thus to the company and/or agent.

The "most likely" future scenario is that the great majority of buyers will pre-screen houses on their own and reduce their search to five or less. Most sellers will have valid information allowing them to have a good idea of the market value of their home. Buyers will have prequalified themselves financially, will be aware of their credit rating, and many will already be pre-approved for a loan. Buyers and sellers will have a fair amount of information regarding all the pieces necessary to complete the transaction.

In this scenario, the agent will provide the emotional and "high touch" services necessary, as well as guidance in allowing the buyer and seller to convert data/information into knowledge/action. The company will provide transaction guidance, follow-up marketing functions and support to the entire transaction to assure that "outstanding total experience."

The "way out" scenario calls for the broker regaining control of the customer through technology. In this scenario, the customer of the broker becomes the consumer, not the agent. To assure a quality experience, some salespersons will be employees, while others may remain as independent contractors. The broker will provide and control all functions related to the transaction. Some will own these service providers directly, while others will create strategic partnerships, branded to the company, to provide them. Many services will be provided by employees rather than independent contractors. Specialization of function in the process will be a hallmark.

Although this scenario was considered "way out," by many focus group participants, it surfaced in virtually all of the focus group sessions and as such may have some real validity. In the author's estimation, it is not "way out," as some of the larger players in the industry seem to be already on that track.

The "extreme" future scenario would have technology providers integrating the entire transaction, parceling out the "high touch" portions to subcontractors for a fee. In this scenario, the future role of the brokerage firm seems to disappear, as the assignments would be made directly to individual agents (or to agent groups), and the real estate company as we know it today would become superfluous.

OWNERSHIP OF TRANSACTIONAL INFORMATION

In the past, the information was the proprietary property of the real estate industry. The MLS was the creator, repository and owner, the consumer the user. At present, ownership of the information has already crossed over to the end user, thanks largely to the Internet. Therefore, there is no longer any value in attempting to keep most information secret or proprietary. Self-imposed barriers are the only ones left preventing consumers from accessing all property, financing and transactional information.

The consensus was unanimous that in any future scenario, self-imposed barriers will altogether disappear and will no longer have any relevance. Information will flow freely and rapidly to all entities who may have use for it.

CAPITAL INVESTMENT REQUIREMENTS

What had traditionally been a rather low capital investment business (a desk, a phone and an MLS book), has already changed to one requiring ever increasing investment. Much present investment capital comes from the bottom line of the company. While an increasing amount of this is being used for technology, investment in expanding and updating offices, creating services and funding acquisitions is creating heavier demands for capital.

In the "likely" future scenario, the need for capital expands even further, as new non-real-estate companies enter the arena and expand services to meet rising consumer demands. Pressure from the public (and from this new competition) to add services increases capital requirements, as does the ongoing need for expansion through acquisition.

A "far out" scenario would have capital investment becoming a strategic imperative leading to more consolidation in the industry. Commission splits will change and be negotiated based on contribution to capital investment.

INCOME AND EXPENSE

There was universal affirmation that in the present scenario there is ever-increasing pressure on the bottom line due to unprofitable commission splits, the tendency of technology expenses to become bottom-line expenses, increased operating expenses and expanded service requirements. This pressure is further exacerbated by lack of management-trained business managers. This has already reached crisis proportions, but the crisis is partially hidden by an ever-growing and expanding economy.

The "likely" future scenario is that commission pricing pressures will continue to grow, as customers do more information gathering and pieces of the transaction formerly consider the real estate professional's role become parceled out to others.

The rapidly changing world of technology moves technology costs from the category of "investments" to "current expenses." The likelihood of an economic turndown increases, and that event will cause numerous companies to close their doors.

On the positive side, better business management, evolutionary changes in commission splits and sharing of investment expenses with salespersons will start to improve bottom-line performance.

The "far out" scenario indicates further industry consolidation because of financial pressures to achieve economy of scale. Brokers will once again regain control of their companies and will provide additional ancillary services for a fee, thus offsetting reduced revenues per transaction from commission income. The bottom line begins to grow. Meanwhile, increased salesperson productivity will cause their income to increase.

The majority of focus group participants believe that as consumers gain direct access to information and perform search and other functions previously done by agents, pressure on commissions paid will increase. Income per transaction will go down, but because of time savings supported by technology, sales agent productivity will increase and their personal bottom-line income will grow.

There was some disagreement regarding total market share, but most believe the brokerage industry share of the total number of transactions will decrease by ten to twenty percent. Some of this decline, however, will be offset by growth from participation in new home sales, as the industry better focuses itself on home builder marketing needs.

In all of the sessions, there seemed to be no unanimity of thinking regarding the unbundling of services and menu-driven pricing, whereby specific fees are attached to specific services provided to the consumer.

However, a majority thought that in the future,

the sales agent will provide core real estate services (listing, showing, negotiating), while the company will provide branded auxiliary services necessary to complete the transaction. These will be additional profit centers for the company. Specialization within the core services is also anticipated, with some agents acting solely as listers, others as negotiators, etc.

INDEPENDENT CONTRACTOR STATUS

There was general agreement that this vehicle has limited usefulness in the markets of the future. Control of the "total customer experience" requires a larger measure of control of service providers than the independent relationship allows. One possibility is a mixed arrangement, where some are independent and some are employees. New services which require no license would undoubtedly be done by employees.

AGENCY

A great deal of confusion reigns here. While the freedom to act without the restrictions of agency is appealing to reduce liability and make things much simpler, there is little doubt that one of the "services" the public values is the ultimate responsibility for actions by the professionals involved in the transaction.

Regardless of issues of who represents whom, accountability to the client will remain a significant value added by the real estate professional. Without this, the public will most likely believe we are worth something less and therefore expect to pay less for our services.

OVERALL VIEW OF
THE INDUSTRY TODAY

While not unanimous, most participants agreed that the real estate brokerage industry today is disjointed, dysfunctional, inefficient and lacks leadership at a time when it crucially needs it.

SOME GUIDELINES FOR
YOUR OWN "FUTURING"

1) Read extensively, and broadly, including your own local newspaper business and financial sections, *The Wall Street Journal*, and publications such as *Forbes, Money* and *Inc.* magazines. Look for parallels between other industries and what is—or should be— going on in the real estate industry.

2) Study other businesses, particularly to discover how they are viewing the consumer. What impact is the changing role of the consumer having on their strategic planning? And, conversely, what impact will the direction of other industries have on the mindset and habits, the wants and desires of the general consumer marketplace? What are the major retailing giants planning? What about the major e-commerce players? How might that affect either consumer demands and habits, or specifically, the way real estate-related services are delivered?

3) In your futuring exercises, focus not so much on whether or not a certain trend will take shape or a certain change will occur. Think rather in

terms of "What If" that happens. After all, we can never determine with any degree of certitude what will actually happen in the future. But we can formulate specific plans regarding what would have to be done if certain things were to occur.

A further test of the validity of a proposed response to a possible future development involves evaluating the effect of the proposed change on your future success should the anticipated development *not* occur.

Consider, for example, the possibility that in the future sales agents will no longer be independent contractors but will be in some form of employee relationship with the firm. Are there changes that you could implement today in your recruiting, hiring and compensation programs that would put you in good stead should that become a future reality—and that would also have a positive impact on your business should it not become the norm?

4) Do not evaluate information, make plans or draw conclusions in a vacuum. Every part of the puzzle must be related to all the other parts in order to see its meaningfulness and develop a plan that will work in the real world. The real world is not compartmentalized. That is one of the challenges of strategic planning and it involves the "chaos" theory of management. In a world where nothing is static and each change precipitates other changes, planning must be equally dynamic.

5) Evaluate every change in direction with an eye to its relationship to your long term plans. Will this change put us in better position when all of the "What Ifs" are considered? Is there another alternative that will cover an even wider range of future scenarios?

6) Do not abandon short-term successes in your search for long-term security. Can we make changes that will position us better for future developments AND without disturbing (and, in fact, actually increasing) our profitability and relevance in the immediate present? This is perhaps one of the greatest challenges to management and one that will separate the long-term winners from those who burn out like rockets in the Fourth of July sky.

THE CIRCLE IS UNENDING

Having traversed this work from Prologue to Conclusion, the bigger picture of the future of the real estate industry is now hopefully in clearer focus.

At this point, having heard the author's "take" on the future and then combining that with the outlook of our focus groups, it might be beneficial to go back and re-read some of the specific material in the individual chapters, this time within the context of all of the issues discussed throughout the book.

Some of the individual pieces of the puzzle may not have seemed to have much validity on first reading. Some you may have rejected out of hand—either because they did not seem to fit the real estate industry as you have experienced it, or because they seemed to relate to a future too "far out" based on the facts as you perceived them at the time.

A classic example occurs frequently in our futuring sessions when we suggest the possibility of a salaried status for sales agents. The immediate reaction can be summarized as follows: "We have enough trouble trying to manage the salaried employees we already have (managers, administrative personnel) and over whom we have some degree of control. How could we ever survive in a salaried mode with agents that we can't control!"

A very valid observation, given the current state of the industry. If all we did was put our existing agents on salary, most of us would indeed go broke (or crazy, or both!). But what if we view the change to a salaried configuration as only a small part of a number of overall changes that may have to occur in order to maintain a meaningful position for the brokerage industry in the marketplace? The position may begin to make some sense.

Are there changes in the qualifications of the people we should be hiring, changes in the job descriptions of our professional staff, changes in the overall compensation and benefit structure of the company and changes in the nature and number of services that we offer (and in the way the consumer compensates us) that, taken together, might make a salaried structure not only a possibility, but also a mandated direction?

The same thought processes can be applied to just about every facet of the business.

Take, for example, the "fee for services" approach, where the functions in the real estate transaction are "unbundled" and services are offered *a la carte* in a menu-driven configuration rather than in the traditional manner, where they are "bundled" and priced as a package. This approach may not make a lot of sense given the current state of the industry. But will this be a valid response to a consumer push for lower fees? And does it fit into emerging patterns of specialization within the real estate brokerage firm?

What effect would a menu-driven delivery system have on our business if a number of the services now considered the unique domain of the real estate practitioner were to be taken over by others—some by consumers themselves, others by "partners" in the transaction (or even by players not yet identified with this business, such as EBay or Wal-Mart for example)? And what implications would this have on the structure of our firm, our hiring practices and compensation plans?

You can see that all of the facets are somehow related, all of the future directions entwined one with another.

Whether the future holds a drastic transformation or just an ongoing evolution of the industry, for most of us the safest way to arrive there successfully will involve a series of small but significant steps. That has always been the case. The difference today and tomorrow involves not only the pacing of those steps but also the direction which they must take.

"You have to know where to plant your feet if you are going to have any kind of a chance at a shot!"